Praise for *Dynamic Communication*

Jill created a body of work that is de~~signed~~
challenge your business might
leadership and public communicatio   rk.
Open any chapter and get in

—EKATERINA WALTER, AUTHOR OF *THE*   ~~~~ BESTSELLER
THINK LIKE ZUCK AND *POWER OF VISUAL STORYTELLING*

Communication is what we all do and most do it so wrong. *Dynamic
Communication* is a must read for every professional, entrepreneur,
and business owner. Jill's years of experience are masterfully
captured in these pages.

—RAMON RAY, FOUNDER AND EDITOR OF *SMART HUSTLE* MAGAZINE

This book cuts straight through the bullshit and reveals
actionable communication strategies, which might change your life
and your business forever. Whether you're just starting or already
managing an empire, *Dynamic Communication* is a must read.

—ILJA GRZESKOWITZ, BESTSELLING AUTHOR, KEYNOTE SPEAKER, AND CHANGE EXPERT

If you're an entrepreneur, you need this book. It is one of the
most comprehensive collections of communications strategies
that I've ever seen—from stage to screen to classroom to
boardroom—and lots more in between.

—MICHELLE VILLALOBOS, PROFESSIONAL SPEAKER, SUPERSTAR BRAND STRATEGIST,
AND FOUNDER OF *THE WOMEN'S SUCCESS SUMMIT*

Of all the communication books out there, this is *the one* you need
to read. No matter where you are in your business or career,
from just starting to growing teams, to managing an empire,
there is a strategy in this book that will help you become a
great communicator—not just a good one.

—SYLVIE DI GIUSTO, FOUNDER OF EXECUTIVE IMAGE CONSULTING AND AUTHOR OF
THE IMAGE OF LEADERSHIP

This book is the definitive go-to guide to get you raised, praised, and promoted in your career, or get you booked solid. In-person, onstage, and online, Jill shows you how to dominate any message and influence any audience so they listen, act, and buy.

—David Newman, Author of *Do It! Marketing*

The ability to communicate effectively is decisive in the business world. Jill's book is like a business communication degree in a single book, and taught in a way that you—business owners, managers, leaders—can actually relate to.

—Eric S. Yuan, CEO and Founder of Zoom Video Communications

Jill Schiefelbein's *Dynamic Communication* blew me away. I'm in the communications world and I found some new strategies that are already making a difference in my business. Implement her incredibly actionable strategies and you'll close more contracts too!

—Kate Delaney, NBC Talk Show Host and Media Consultant

Love, love, LOVE the straight from the gut raw and REAL approach laid out here. If you're serious about communication and growth in business, not just professionally but also in terms of how it impacts on you personally, then you *must* get this book!

—Kat Loterzo, Bestselling Author and Success Mentor to Entrepreneurs, Leaders, and Creatives

Jill puts her finger on the important but subtle, non-obvious communication tricks. These might be intuitive for some people, but for the rest of us, it's a huge benefit to pay more attention to the techniques she's laid out for us here. Highly recommended.

—Andy Crestodina, Co-Founder of Orbit Media and Author of *Content Chemistry*

Specific communication skills are the key to everything. It's what will help you grow your business and your career. This book is filled with bite-sized nuggets of wisdom. Modern day business owners *and* employees have a blueprint for growth in their hands.

—Jess Todtfeld, Guinness World Record Holder and Author of *Media Secrets*

DYNAMIC COMMUNICATION

27 STRATEGIES TO GROW, LEAD, & MANAGE YOUR BUSINESS

JILL SCHIEFELBEIN

Entrepreneur
PRESS®

Entrepreneur Press, Publisher
Cover Design: Andrew Welyczko
Production and Composition: Eliot House Productions

This publication is designed to provide accurate and authoritative information
in regard to the subject matter covered. It is sold with the understanding that
the publisher is not engaged in rendering legal, accounting or other professional
services. If legal advice or other expert assistance is required, the services of a
competent professional person should be sought.

Library of Congress Cataloging-in-Publication Data
    Names: Schiefelbein, Jill, author.
    Title: Dynamic communication: strategies to grow, lead, and manage your
       business / Jill Schiefelbein.
    Description: Irvine, California : Entrepreneur Press, 2017.
    Identifiers: LCCN 2016054461 (print) | LCCN 2017004584 (ebook) | ISBN
       978-1-59918-608-5 (paperback) | ISBN 1-59918-608-X (paperback) |
       ISBN 978-1-61308-365-9
    Subjects: LCSH: Business communication. | Industrial management.
       | Leadership. | BISAC: BUSINESS & ECONOMICS / Business
       Communication / General. | BUSINESS & ECONOMICS /
       Entrepreneurship. | REFERENCE / Personal & Practical Guides. |
       BUSINESS & ECONOMICS / Skills.
    Classification: LCC HF5718 .S286 2017 (print) | LCC HF5718 (ebook) |
       DDC 658.4/5—dc23
    LC record available at https://lccn.loc.gov/2016054461

Printed in the United States of America

20 19 18 17   10 9 8 7 6 5 4 3 2 1

To the best entrepreneurs I know—my parents. Though you may not profit monetarily, you created and developed two great products. For that, I'm immeasurably thankful.

Contents

PART III

Marketing That Educates

Creating Value-Filled, Magnetic Marketing

PART IV

Oh, the Humanity!

Public Communication Strategies That Help You Connect

CHAPTER 11

Surround Yourself with the Right People:

CHAPTER 12

Hot Off the Presses: *Media, Stories, and*

CHAPTER 13

When the Sh*t Hits the Fan: *Communicating*

PART V

Speak Out, Speak Up

Giving Presentations That Inspire Action

CHAPTER 14

How to Not Suck on Stage: *Delivery*

Contents

CHAPTER 27

Six Steps for Innovation: *Cultivating*
Intrapreneurship. **245**

CONCLUSION

Slapping a Bandage on It Doesn't Work **255**

Index **259**

Foreword

By Jay Baer

You've no doubt been exposed to the question "if a tree falls in the forest, and there is nobody there to hear it, does it still make a sound?"

It was first pondered—at least in print—in 1710 by philosopher George Berkeley in *A Treatise Concerning the Principles of Human Knowledge*. Perhaps unintentionally, Berkeley's thought experiment also predicted the future. More than 300 years later, "does it still make a sound?" may be more relevant than ever.

In today's world, we are besieged by communication. Long and short. Fast and slow. Writing, audio, photo, video, nonverbal, interpretive dance, puppet shows, social media, and countless other forms.

But how much of it matters? How much of the present tidal wave of communication is relevant or successful by any measure? On average, a staggering 300 HOURS of video are uploaded to YouTube every minute of every day. Yet, only a few videos break out from the *de-facto* "so what?" to reach more people than fit in a living room.

To be successful, communication must create behavior. This has always been so. But today, so much of our communication is vaporous and vapid; not a whiff of motivation to be found.

Like you, I am immersed in this problem. I run a strategy firm that helps the world's most interesting brands solve their communication challenges; and own a media company that produces dozens of pieces of communication each week.

I've been a professional communicator for almost 25 years, and if there's one discovery about which I have no doubt, it is this: as society increases its collective communications volume, the value and effectiveness of that communication declines even more quickly, on a per-piece basis.

Our embrace of "more is better" in communication has spawned a classic corkscrew effect whereby the more we communicate, the worse we communicate. And because our communication is less successful, we decide to remediate by communicating more often and in more ways. Which, in turn, lessens the impact of communication further, and the cycle repeats.

We are spiraling into the ground, one crappy blog post, pointless email, narcissistic video, and inscrutable emoji at a time.

Until now.

You are about to go on a journey. A journey that will make you a manifestly better communicator. My friend Jill Schiefelbein has created a wholly modern and eyes-wide-open book about today's communication landscape. And you couldn't find a better person to guide you on this journey.

Jill is a true 360-degree communicator. People (mostly in Hollywood, I presume) say that actor/singer/dancer is the "triple threat" of the entertainment business. Jill is the triple threat (and then some) of communication. Whether it's in a classroom, on stage, behind the microphone, and now in a book, Jill is the embodiment of a dynamic communicator.

You'll discover it for yourself in these pages.

Dynamic Communication wasn't written as a text book per se, but it should be required reading for every student in every college or university in the United States. Freshman year, before bad habits related to a high school career spent texting and communicating primarily through the distorted prism of Snapchat are calcified for life.

While you read *Dynamic Communication*, I want you to make notes on the elements of the book you like best. Will you do that for me, please? I'm very interested to know if you and I appreciate the very same components, or if I am markedly more enthusiastic, or cynical, than you are. At any point as you read the book, send me an email at Jay@JayBaer.com—yes, that's my real email address. Let me know if you concur with the following.

Six Reasons I'm Telling My Friends About *Dynamic Communication*

1. *No Candy.* Jill pulls no punches in this book. She tells you exactly why communication is broken, and shines a tiki torch on the traps you may have encountered in your communications past. I hate books that treat readers like toddlers, telling them on each page, "even if you do this wrong, it will all be okay in the end." It won't be okay. Bad communication doesn't yield fairy tale endings, and I love that Jill doesn't promise any.

2. *Expert Advice.* What Jill has forgotten about communication would fill a book—or at least an overlong pamphlet. But she knows one of the unspoken keys to communication success: everyone's a teacher, and everyone's a student. She doesn't have to be the instructor on every page. Instead, Jill includes counsel from many of the world's best communicators throughout the book, like my friend David Newman on webinar success. Valuable teachings!

3. *Medicine You Want to Drink.* You would think that a book on communication would be well-written and pleasure to read, right? I wish that were always the case. But, I've read several books about effective communication that were themselves ineffective. Oh, the irony! Fortunately, you won't have to endure

that here, as *Dynamic Communication* is sharp, brisk, and clear, (which sounds vaguely like the name of an indie-rock album).

4. *A Go-To Reference.* My favorite business books are those that are easy to skim AFTER you've read it the first time. I want a book that I can easily refer back to when I need to remember exactly what to do in a particular situation or circumstance. Jill has organized the material here in that very practical way. I guarantee this is a book you'll keep at the ready even after you've read it.

5. *Organization Scheme.* I don't know that I've ever seen a book that organizes its teachings around communication type. Presentations. Managing teams. Soliciting and giving feedback. Marketing communication. Sales communication. It's a very smart way to avoid lumping too many concepts together and making them indistinguishable. I've written five books, and have never even considered doing it this way. I love the structure of this book.

6. *Tactical Coverage.* This is not a book about communication theory. Jill touches on it, of course, but this is above all a working person's book on communication best practices. As such, it provides specific recommendations for how to succeed with today's key communication formats like sales scripts, live video, press releases, meeting agendas, and dozens more. Incredibly useful!

I am thrilled that you've chosen to dive in to *Dynamic Communication*. It's a book that's needed more than ever, and congratulations to Jill Schiefelbein for bringing it to life.

Your communicating friend,

Jay Baer, President of Convince & Convert, and author of *Hug Your Haters*, Bloomington, Indiana, January, 2017

Preface

'm an educator at heart. I care about sharing information in a way that can be applied and used to make a positive difference. Theory is great, but it's nothing without application.

Application is my zenith.

After teaching communication courses at a university for 11 years, it was frustrating for me to see how students could memorize and regurgitate information for a test, but were not able to apply what they learned to their lives. I finally realized where I could make my impact—strategies for understanding communication in business that could be applied to increase efficiencies, enhance relationships, and impact the bottom line. Thus, *Dynamic Communication* was born.

This book contains 27 actionable strategies that you can use to implement dynamic communication in your organization. While the chapters and strategies are organized sequentially, each one is designed to be accessed individually as well. While you'll benefit from having read previous chapters, you'll still be able to execute a specific strategy just by reading that section on its own.

In each chapter, I also shine a spotlight on a successful entrepreneur or entrepreneurial thinker who provides great insights on how to grow, lead, and manage your business. I interviewed dozens of brilliant minds to curate this content, and their contributions make this book even more valuable. You'll find these in the "Real People. Real Stories. Real Results" segments. The full videos of each interview are available on the book website at www.dynamiccommunicationbook.com—over 12 hours of great conversations about business, communication, and everything in between.

Whenever possible, I refer back to previous chapters with "Flashback" sections and indicate "Spoiler Alert" pop-outs to draw your attention to related future chapters. My goal with this book is to make the theoretical tangible. In other words, I want to give you the knowledge you need to drive growth, create and manage happier workplaces, and be a better leader.

I encourage you to mark the heck out of this book. Grab a highlighter. Get a pen. Sharpen a pencil. And at the end of each chapter make a note of one thing—just one—you want to make sure you remember. Write these in the book or get a separate notebook. Better yet, download the free accompanying workbook at www.dynamiccommunicationbook.com. Either way, by the end of the book you'll have 27 ways to make your business communication more dynamic, with ideas that can actually be applied to produce positive change.

I hope you'll consider me the business communication professor you wish you had.

INTRODUCTION

Why "Good Communication Skills" Aren't Enough

Misunderstandings and missed opportunities—these are the consequences of poor communication. And these undesirable results carry a high cost to you and your business.

As humans, we often take our ability to communicate for granted. We assume that when we write or speak, people listen in the way most beneficial to us, in a way that will get us the results we want.

But all you have to do is go back to your childhood to see how simple communication can get ridiculously misconstrued.

Remember the game of telephone you played as a kid? You sit in a circle, and one person whispers a phrase to the person to her right. That person repeats what he heard to the person on his right, and so on until the message makes it all the way around the circle. By the time the last person to hear the message whispers it to the person who started it, laughter ensues, because it's nothing like what was originally said.

Every day in business, your employees, your consumers, and the general population are playing a game of telephone with your brand.

When you think about how distorted messages can get when filtering through the ears and minds of the masses, it's almost terrifying. How can you—a business owner, a manager, a leader—ensure that your messages are received in the way and manner you want them to be received? And how can you be sure the time spent strategizing and crafting your communication and marketing yields the results you desire?

That's what this book is written to address.

No matter how well-scripted, well-meaning, and well-spoken your business communication is, there is always room for interpretation. However, you can minimize your risk of misinterpretation by understanding communication as part of a larger combination of interactions and engagements that need to be consistent to be successful.

Communication is more than words. It's more than messages. It's more than speaking. It's more than writing.

When people say they have "great communication skills," they are typically referring to one or more of the above abilities. Job advertisements and recruiters often ask for "excellent written and verbal communication skills" from candidates.

Just because you can write a grammatically correct, coherent proposal, essay, or email doesn't mean you have good written communication skills, and just because you can do a presentation without using "ums" and "uhs" doesn't mean you're a good verbal communicator.

Successful, dynamic communication is measured by the actions and results you generate—not the messages you produce.

Let's take a look at what dynamic communication really is.

Dynamic Communication—What You Really Need

There are literally hundreds of definitions for the word *communication*. When most people think of communication, they think of two people sending messages to each other or one person sending a message to a group. At a base level, communication is the transmission of information from one person to another, or one person to the masses. A thought, an idea, a feeling—some piece of information is shared.

But as most of us know from having a message misinterpreted, just because you intend to communicate something doesn't mean that's the way it's received. Similarly, the decision to *not* communicate is, in fact, communication!

Everything you say, and everything you don't say, communicates. But communication is so much more than words and messages. Your actions, and your inactions, communicate as well. In fact, one cannot not communicate. What you don't say matters just as much as, if not more than, what you do say.

I wish I could claim I came up with the phrase "one cannot not communicate," but, alas, it is not mine. So where did it come from? This idea is one of the five original axioms of the communications field presented by Watzlawick, Beavin, and Jackson in their 1967 work Pragmatics of Human Communication.

When I used to teach business communication at Arizona State University, I'd toss this axiom out to my students on the first day of class and we'd debate it. By the end of class, students would have thrown out every idea imaginable that a person could do to not communicate and find that, in fact, not communicating IS communicating!

I often use (and of course cite; I'm a good recovering academic, after all) this phrase at the beginning of my programs and speeches, because it's important to know that the decision to not communicate does, in fact, communicate. So does a lack of consistency in communication. I'll touch more on this in future chapters.

To repeat what I've already said: Communication is more than words.

And to be a good communicator—a dynamic communicator—you need more than words to get action. A dynamic communicator is confident, adaptable, progressive, proactive, and stimulating. A dynamic communicator commands an audience, leads a team, presents ideas, generates sales, achieves buy-in, and delivers results. Dynamic communication is communication that lives beyond the words and provides residual impacts. *Dynamic communication generates action.*

If you want your communication to drive business growth, increase the bottom line, retain talented employees, secure investors, attract new customers, and enhance your brand image, you need to understand that your words and actions communicate well beyond the initial recipients.

Communicating to One Audience Isn't Enough

When it comes to business, for your communication to be truly dynamic and generate real, sustained action and results, you must realize that it simultaneously impacts three audiences.

Yes. Three.

See, business doesn't happen in a bubble. Each business is part of a bigger system (the global economy), and each business is also its own system with multiple moving parts.

Because of this, you need to strategize and execute communication across three audiences to produce maximum results. They are:

1. Internal—your employees and contract partners
2. External—the general public, media, and interested parties
3. Consumer—your sales audience and client base

All the strategies presented in this book have a direct or indirect impact on these three audiences. Before diving into the strategies, though, allow me to explain why it's important that we understand communication as simultaneously impacting these three audiences.

Three Simultaneous Dynamics, One Giant System

Bear with me while I put on my proverbial professor hat and share a little bit about systems, but in a way that won't put you to sleep.

Confession: I love systems theory. In fact, if I were to create my own "I (heart) something" T-shirt, it would be "I (heart) systems." When I learned about it as an undergraduate, it was the first time I thought, "Wow, this is going to be good for more than regurgitation on a quiz," and paid attention.

When I was studying communication theory and researching the flow of information in and out of terrorist camps (really, that did happen), I got to see this theory in action for the first time.

If you Google it, you'll see many different interpretations and applications of systems theory. Here's how to understand it, in simple terms, for understanding and improving communication and growing, leading, and managing your business.

A presumably smart dude named Ludwig von Bertalanffy, a biologist, proposed an idea that was counter to the then-current thinking in 1928 that in science we can isolate variables, break things into components, look at them in a vacuum, and then put them in their proper place in a system.

OK. That was a lot of textbook-style jargon. Think of it this way. The human body is a system. And let's say this system experiences a heart attack. Under the old way of thinking, if someone had a heart attack, scientists would isolate the heart as a component of the system (the body) and try to figure out what went wrong. In this approach, a doctor would look only at the heart, find the problem, fix it, put it back into the body, and expect it to function like a well-oiled machine.

We know that this is not how the body works. There are a lot of different reasons someone has a heart attack, and by not looking at the heart as one of many subsystems within the body, which all impact the heart's function, you can't figure out the true origins of a heart attack.

Make sense?

Bertalanffy thought so. He challenged the status quo, said, "This is ridiculous," and proposed a new way of thinking. In looking at the body (the system) as being made up of many organs (subsystems) that all operate together to achieve a goal (living), you realize that while the heart physically beating is a sign of life, there are a lot of things that need to happen for the heart to be able to beat.

That idea is known as interdependence—that all the pieces that exist are mutually reliant on the others. In other words, the whole is greater than the sum of its parts. But without any of the parts, it wouldn't operate the same, if at all.

In this same sense, every business is a system with many subsystems. Traditionally, these are thought of as departments or teams, but your customers and the general public are also part of your business system.

Think about it—in order for a (larger) business to run smoothly you need to have variations on a management team, a human resources team, a financial team, a sales team, a research team, a support team, a development team, and many others. If you think of your business in terms of systems theory, every department—every subsystem—impacts the others. If your sales team, for example, isn't producing results, you can't fix the problem just by focusing on the sales team. The sales team operates within a system with many parts, and all these parts interact together to create the end result.

Think of the different subsystems in a startup software business. A development team can't get funding to continue work if there isn't a sales team in place to generate revenue and a support team in place to help the end user. A sales team can't succeed without a product to sell to potential consumers. And the business will never get funding if it can't demonstrate a market demand for the software through needs analysis and then use strong marketing and branding to increase that demand.

Do you see the three audiences at play here? Here's a story to illustrate.

I was approached by a VP of sales engineering at a company that created a software solution for the financial services industry; the software monitored social media posts from employees to ensure they did not violate any compliance regulations. He came to me requesting presentation-skills training for his sales engineers, who were becoming more client-facing in the sales life cycle. Essentially, he wanted his engineers to be able to better communicate to potential consumers, and he thought presentation-skills training was the way to make that happen.

He was focused on communication impacts to the consumer audience.

I can conduct a training session on presentation skills any day. However, I also knew that, since communication does not just impact one audience, there was a more holistic solution that would generate better long-term results and lead to more dynamic communication. So I asked him a series of questions to understand the other two audiences at play.

It turned out that the sales team had the highest turnover rate of any department in the company. This meant that whenever the sales engineers went into the field with a sales representative to talk to a potential client, they never knew with whom they would be paired. No matter how much the sales engineers' presentation skills improved, the internal issue of turnover and inconsistent pairing still existed and would hinder maximum results.

To achieve better results, the internal audience *also needs to be addressed.*

After probing further, I learned that recently the company's software solution had shifted from an on-site, installed solution to a cloud-based solution. However, the support team, which was the first point of contact for general inquiry questions about the product or post-purchase support, was highly focused on IT solutions and used to speaking to a computer systems external public. In order to really drive bottom-line change, another shift was needed.

The external audience *perception of the company and its products needs a communication shift.*

Addressing any one of these audiences would lead to small gains. But for long-term, sustained results, the communication dynamics in all three audiences—consumer, internal, and external—needed to be addressed.

Rinse and Repeat

Let's review the stage that we've set for the rest of this book. Communication is more than words and messages. It's more than transferring data or information from one person to another. And in business, thinking that you are communicating to just one audience is not the reality. You need dynamic communication—communication that is action-oriented, results-focused, adaptable, and comprehensive.

If you want your business communication strategy to work, you need to take three audiences into consideration—internal, external, and consumer. Your business is a system with many parts, and it operates in a larger ecosystem with multiple competitors. In order to thrive, you have to make sure your communication across each of these audiences is in sync. Inconsistency in messaging, perception, and action can hinder your ability to grow.

Misunderstandings and missed opportunities—these are the residual effects of poor communication.

The 27 dynamic communication strategies in this book are presented for you to implement in your business. Whether you're an entrepreneur just starting out and trying to grow your business, the head of a company seeking to create a stellar culture where your employees enjoy coming to work, or an organizational leader striving to impact and influence those with whom you interact, this book is for you.

In each chapter, we'll dive into the nuances of different aspects of business and workplace communication and introduce strategies you can use for immediate results.

Sound good? Great.

Let's get dynamic!

Stuff to Read So You Sound Smart: The (Simplified) History of Organizational Communication

If you're not interested in how people have studied communication in businesses and organizations in the past and how it's evolved over time, and you're really just getting this book to dive into the strategies, skip this section and move full steam ahead. Really. I won't be offended.

But if you're still considering your next move, having a fundamental understanding of the evolution of communication in the workplace and how management practices have changed and developed over time will help you in determining how you grow your business, manage your teams, and lead within your organization.

Still with me? Excellent. You're now in my communication classroom. And here's your first lesson.

When communication emerged as a field of study, the first model that was created was quite simple. It was "a sender sent a message to a receiver." Transmission of information from A to B. It doesn't get more basic than that. And within organizations, there was a specific hierarchy that dictated the direction of communication. This became known as bureaucracy (and a dude named Max Weber spearheaded this movement).

Now we know communication is not that simple. Yet many businesses still run this way today. A sender (typically a boss) sends a message (typically an order) to a receiver (typically an employee). The boss expects that the employee is motivated by a paycheck, wants to keep his job, and will follow directions.

We also know that type of manager doesn't keep employees around for long.

If you want to sound smart when talking about this management style, you can reference the beginnings of organization management theories. This is where Frederick Taylor's scientific management theory comes into play. Back in the 1880s, Taylor started to present these ideas. He believed there was one best way to do every task and that each business would discover this through time and motion studies. It's then assumed that the boss knows best, orders employees, and if you don't follow directions you're easily replaced. Because you're just a cog in the wheel of the organizational machine.

Sounds like a great organization to work for, right?

Now, in some cases this style of management is necessary: military organizations, life-or-death processes, mixing dangerous chemicals, etc. But for most companies, when it comes to managing your people on a day-to-day basis, treating them like cogs in a wheel isn't the way to retain employees.

So then companies started to open up a little bit and realize that (gasp) employees also had a voice, and they wanted to be treated as individuals with hopes and dreams and fears and needs.

It seems obvious now. But up to the early 1920s it wasn't, until a guy named Elton Mayo came along and went to the Hawthorne Works (a Western Electric factory) outside Chicago. He was a researcher hired to increase the productivity of the plant—basically, they wanted him to do time and motion studies to determine the best way and conditions in which to reach optimum output.

So Mayo and his team came in, met with management, and decided to tinker with some conditions to see if they would affect productivity. They fiddled with the amount of lighting in the factory, and productivity increased. They played with giving workers different break times, and productivity increased. They decided to bring in food at breaks, and productivity increased. With most changes they saw a corresponding change in productivity—more often than not an increase.

The researchers were baffled. According to time and motion principles, there was only supposed to be one best way to do every task, but that clearly wasn't the case here.

What they found was that the workers' productivity increased with each change because they realized that management was paying attention to them. This became known as the Hawthorne Effect.

This paved the way for a long-overdue movement—human relations and resources. And with this movement more parts of the communication model started to be recognized: that employees have a voice and communication can go both ways, that the channel through which a message is delivered plays a role, and the concept of noise.

Not noise as in physical noise, but noise as something that— whether audible or mental—affects the communication process. Physical noise, obviously, blocks out sound and can interrupt messages. But hierarchical noise—noise based on power and positioning—can mentally impact the interpretation of messages, too. Like when you get called into the principal's office and already start bracing yourself for the message you are about to receive. Or your parents yell out your full name (first, middle, and last). Or, in the case of business, a boss asks you to come to her office. That's hierarchical noise. Oh, and there's semantic noise—which is basically noise based on accent, or rate of speech, or incorrect pronunciation, or overuse of jargon. Basically the way someone says something impacts the way you hear or listen to what they have to say.

But there was some hesitation to accept this movement. Bosses and managers had to (gasp) listen to employees, and they realized that taking feedback from employees could actually help their organizations. But that meant they weren't the only people with bright ideas. This simultaneously amazed and threatened them, and some of them acted out. Managers and bosses became fearful. Those newly formed HR teams had their work cut out for them. And worker protection laws started to change. Managers were still treating employees as cogs, but employees were now starting to push back.

This tension gave rise to (as you now know) my favorite period in organizational management—systems theory. The organization as a whole is only as good as its parts. The emphasis on teamwork was highlighted in many studies during this time, and communication eventually adjusted.

Having employees see their role in the bigger picture of an organization is critical to success. There have been many other studies of management and leadership: some good, some bad, some ugly. Most of them are overcomplicated in how they're explained.

Here's what you really need to know. When it comes to communication breakdowns in an organization, you can typically attribute them to one or more elements of the communication model, stemming from a management or leadership style. It could be too much one-way communication, ineffective feedback, improper use or choice of channel, too much noise, a non-optimal environment or context, or what we're about to discover in the first strategy chapter: a grave error in overlooking communication history.

Sound simple?

In many ways it is. But nothing involving people is ever simple.

We have different experiences and points of view. We have different struggles and expectations. We have different talents and interests. And we have different personalities and backgrounds that can both help and hinder organizational progress.

The following 27 chapters contain strategies that you can use to grow, lead, and manage your business. They all have the capacity for massive, positive change. However, they aren't one-size-fits-all. As you read, think of how each one fits into your business, and with your audiences. Use the workbook available at www.dynamiccommunicationbook.com to help your communication become more dynamic.

The Bare Basics

Things You Need to Understand About

Communication

What You Don't Know Can Hurt You

Perceptions and Reality

Before you even think about selling, you need to know what your potential clients and customers know, or think they know.

If you read the introduction, you understand where noise fits into the communication landscape and how damaging it can be to your strategic efforts. In the current economy, we are inundated with information (and misinformation). This is noise that can impact your communication strategy.

There is more information accessible today than at any point in recorded history. I, personally, think that is a good thing. I'm a fan of being able to access information. But with great power comes great responsibility. The problem with the amount of available information is that people are conflating information with knowledge. I call this the knowledge gap, and it's bigger now than ever. Acknowledging that this gap exists, though, is the first step to understanding how to communicate through the noise.

Let's take a deeper look at the knowledge gap and how it presents both challenges and opportunities to entrepreneurs and entrepreneurial thinkers.

The Knowledge Gap

With the number of websites nearing a billion, and search volume reaching more than 50,000 searches per second, the world is inundated with information and the ability to access it.

The phrase "information at your fingertips" is even outdated, as voice searching and commands increase our ability to search and retrieve information on any subject.

What this presents to our society, and to your business economy, is an employee, public, and consumer base that can view as much information about you and your company as you can. But, as we are aware, not all information published is accurate. And simply reading something does not mean that you *know* something.

There is a widening gap between information and knowledge. The gap itself isn't the problem; it's that people confuse information for knowledge. When people mistake information for knowledge, they often make decisions based on misreported or misrepresented data, or from only a small spectrum of information that they've retrieved. A key example of how this often plays out? Media.

The media perpetuates the information and knowledge gap when it reports only part of the information picture. This is common practice and is not likely to change. But the reporting of information is not the real problem. Again, the problem comes when viewers or readers mistake the information for a complete picture or for knowledge.

Information is data—facts, figures, statistics, anecdotes, testimonials, etc.—that is used to *inform* decisions. Knowledge is verified information placed into a context, which can be *applied* to make decisions.

Knowledge Is Information, Applied

The difference between being informed and being able to apply that information lies in one's ability to put theory into practice. Many college students can pass a multiple choice test on game theory from reading a textbook, but ask those same students to use game theory to help foreign policy officials solve a conflict between two feuding nations, and you're likely to get a lot of stumped looks.

That's the difference between information and knowledge.

Helping people bridge that gap can help you win friends and influence people (a nod to Mr. Carnegie there). Not to mention

REAL PEOPLE, REAL STORIES, REAL RESULTS

Jay Baer

CEO and Founder, Convince & Convert, Author of *Youtility* and *Hug Your Haters*

Every Instance of Communication Does Not Equal a Sales Opportunity

The biggest communication mistake that business owners make is the belief that every piece of communication is a sales opportunity. Stop trying to be amazing, and start being useful. Stop trying to create something that magically creates virality. Start trying to be useful, creating things that add real value. That's *Youtility*.

Youtility Equals Useful, Valuable Marketing

Youtility is marketing so useful, people would pay for it. It's marketing with so much intrinsic and inherent value that people would kick in a few bucks to support it. It's marketing that people actually want instead of marketing that people simply tolerate. There's an enormous difference between marketing people want and marketing people don't hate.

It's Not About Speed and Virality

People think the secret to marketing is to be faster, but the reality is the relationships that we build with prospective clients develop more slowly in a series of micro-interactions that take place consistently over time. You have to embrace the power of eventually. *Youtility* is about help, not hype. It's giving information snacks to sell knowledge meals. Take everything you know, and give it away in small pieces.

Give Everything You Know Away

Many people worry that if they give away all this they won't get hired. That's just not true. A list of ingredients doesn't make someone a chef. Holding on to your knowledge and putting gates in front of it is a self-defeating proposition. It's self-defeating to hold your cards that close to the vest. Give away information snacks to sell knowledge meals.

There's Power In Giving, and In Educating

Relationships are built with information first, and people second. If your information is good enough, you'll be allowed to graduate to a telephonic relationship, not before. This is the exact opposite of how business used to be done. There is a lot of power in self-serve information. There's power in giving information away and allowing people to access it. The more you teach, the more audience you'll attract. If people have to call you to buy from you, you're doing it wrong in the knowledge age.

When You Focus on *Youtility*, Competition Doesn't Exist

There is no such thing as competition—there are just partners you haven't done a deal with yet.

it can bring you more business. But how do you know if the gap exists, and, if it does, how do you need to address it? Moreover, how do we bridge that gap without offending or patronizing someone by telling them they don't really know what they're talking about (although in many cases you want to)? The answer: education and empowerment. By empowering consumers to educate themselves, we all win. We bridge that gap. We rise above the noise.

To rise above the noise, you need to first know what noise exists. To do that, you need to get a clear understanding of communication history and how it

SPOILER ALERT

In Chapter 4 we'll talk about how you can better understand the knowledge gap and how it impacts your sales conversations by looking at how others are listening to you. And in Chapters 7 and 8 we'll look at some different education and empowerment strategies that you can use to rise above the noise.

plays into all interactions you have as a business owner, manager, and leader.

Communication History

With each and every person with whom you interact, or with whom you may never interact, you have a communication history. Your communication history consists of all impressions, interactions, messages, information, applications, interactions, and perceptions that someone has or has seen or has experienced of you, your company, or your product/service. A communication history is already established before you get an email, phone call, or meeting—sometimes before you even get a hit on your website.

Consumers are coming to your door armed with an arsenal of information. Likely, someone calling you for a sales discussion or product demo has already done multiple levels of research. In fact, more than 80 percent of consumers do online research prior to any purchase. What this means is that consumers are mining for information, and whatever they find becomes part of your communication history.

The research that makes up the communication history between the potential consumer and the company is largely based on your digital footprint. Your website, social media channels, appearances and media outlets, consumer reviews, and mentions of your company all compose your digital footprint and your brand.

Based on how you appear in all these channels, an expectation is already set in the potential customer's mind. It's important to understand what this impression is so you can adapt your communication appropriately and proactively take any steps you need to clean up any communication history they might have found (see Figure 1–1 on page 8).

Think of these questions:

⊙ What impressions, information, or experiences have other consumers had with your company?

⊙ What digital footprint (your website, social media, review sites, blogs, media mentions, non-owned information) does your company and/or product have?

Potential Customer

{ Business Owner/Leadership
Salesperson
Other Employees
Product or Service
Industry
Similar Companies

FIGURE 1-1

Sources of Communication History for Your Potential Customer

⊙ What similar companies or services exist, and what perception does your desired consumer audience have of these?

Communication is a two-way street. But not all communication is intentional. Your potential customers can be establishing a communication history with you that you really do not want. A negative online review, for example, will be weighing on the customer's mind from the beginning of any conversation you have. That's why it's important to understand the communication history so you can address those concerns and alleviate any fears right off the bat.

Likewise, potential consumers will search for your employees prior to sales conversations or support conversations. Your employees' social media presences and profiles, then, also form part of the communication history. How your employees portray themselves and their relationship to your company online also goes into the communication history, your company's

SPOILER ALERT

Another way to address the elephant in the room (the negative review) is discussed in Chapter 19, when we dive into effective and efficient meetings.

digital footprint, and the impression that potential customers have about your business, your people, your products, and your services.

Here are some questions to ask so that you know what communication history patterns you've already established with a potential client before you get into the heart of a conversation:

- ⊙ Is there something about our business that made you call us over a competitor?
- ⊙ What have you heard about our business prior to this conversation?
- ⊙ What do you feel we will be able to help you with?
- ⊙ What products are you most interested in learning about?
- ⊙ What goals do you have for our conversation today?
- ⊙ How may I best be of assistance?
- ⊙ Have you done any research on other options?
- ⊙ Did you see any case studies on our website? If so, what interested you the most?

All these questions will help you establish the communication history the prospective customer brings to the table. Knowing this, you can eliminate potential problems and get down to business.

Turning a negative communication history around can take some time. And with each conversation, each consumer interaction, and each time the consumer interacts with your online brand identity, pieces are added to the big puzzle that is your communication history. This is one reason it is so important to take copious notes on your customer conversations, as it keeps a track record of your communication history. This also makes a customer feel more loyal to the company and helps retain clients.

This is also why customer relationship management (CRM) software is so popular. Aside from tracking the customer's lifestyle, it allows you to keep a full record of the communication history in a database that can be accessible by anyone, so that when you're unavailable the customer still remains top priority. Communication history is more than birthdays and spouse names. It's more than product and order and support history. It's the whole picture that allows you or anyone in your company to serve the customer at the best and highest possible level.

Knowing as much of the communication history puzzle as you can will help you better serve the customer, meet their needs and expectations, and retain clients. It also impacts your greater communication strategy and allows you to be more proactive in all your consumer interactions. It allows you to rise above the noise and figure out how you may best empower and educate your potential consumer base, provide value, and leave dynamic impressions.

⊙ ⊙ ⊙

In the next chapter we'll talk about how you can manage a negative communication history and put people at ease by reducing any uncertainty that exists and being clearer in your messaging.

Don't Make Things Awkward

Reduce Uncertainty and Proactively Communicate

If you ever took a communication course, you probably have a vague recollection of uncertainty reduction theory. Many of the foundational theories in most fields have a large application in a business context. This is one of them. So I'm going to break it down for you, piece by piece, so you can see why it's important to understand the role proactive, dynamic communication plays in reducing uncertainty in business environments and how it can actually help you increase productivity with your employees and grow your sales numbers.

Reducing Uncertainty

In 1975 two guys (Charles Berger and Richard Calabrese) thought it would be cool to come up with a theory to describe initial interactions between people. They thought, "Hmmm . . . how can we figure out what type of information people need to feel comfortable when interacting with another person—and how do people try to find out this information?"

In other words, before I spill the beans in any conversation, what information do I need to have to feel comfortable and safe with the other person? This is probably why the theory is also known as initial interaction theory. Clearly, theorists aren't too creative with names. I'd prefer "how to know if I want to get in (metaphorical) bed with someone theory" over "uncertainty reduction theory" . . . but I digress.

So these guys created a few experiments, sent out some surveys, and found out a lot of information that helps us understand the information-seeking and gathering experience that people partake in prior to an "initial synchronous communication." And they found some good stuff that I'll share with you in this chapter.

If those terms are new to you, *synchronous communication* is communication that takes place in real time (video chat, phone call, face-to-face conversation). *Asynchronous communication* is communication that takes place at different time intervals (text, email, handwritten letters, discussion forum posts).

Now, when this theory was created, no one was using Snapchat or Facebook. We weren't texting or video-chatting. And almost no one was using email. Heck, cell phones weren't around and you had to memorize numbers or look in an antiquated object called a phone book. So the initial interaction held a lot of weight. A lot. The only way you could've had pre-interactions that were asynchronous was through snail mail or a fax machine, if you had a fancy office.

Now, though, we have access to tons of information, and even asynchronous exchanges, before you have a synchronous conversation with someone. The biggest reducer of uncertainty in our lives today is Google. And your customers, employees, potential employees, and potential investors are actively using it.

The reason people want to reduce uncertainty is so we can predict actions

FLASHBACK

Think back to Chapter 1 on communication history— the reason people gather information about you and your company is to help reduce their uncertainty about you.

and behaviors. If you think about it, this is important for safety, sanity, and general all-around well being.

So what you need to know, in order to be a dynamic communicator, is that people are reducing their uncertainty about you before you may even know that they are looking into you.

According to the smart theorist dudes, there are three strategies we use to gather information about someone: passive, active, and interactive. Let's look at each one and why they matter.

Passive Uncertainty Reduction

When the original theory was created, passive information gathering was done by observation. It was basically like spying on someone or observing them in their natural habitat (when the person didn't know they were being watched). Today, that takes the form of due diligence research and information seeking online. Now we can find reviews on companies or people, look at LinkedIn profiles, search other social media sites, watch videos, and search images—in other words, we can be complete and total creepers.

Active Uncertainty Reduction

Active means for reducing uncertainty were originally things like asking a friend or trusted colleague. This type of information gathering still happens. Have you ever posted on Facebook to see if any of your connections have a referral for a repair service? I know I have—there's comfort in knowing that someone else you know has worked with a business. It reduces uncertainty. Active strategies also happen directly with the business. If you want to see how responsive a company is before taking a meeting, it's easy to test responsiveness on social media by commenting or sending a tweet. If potential consumers, employees, or investors are doing this, you'd better hope you're responsive. Not responding communicates and increases uncertainty to the point where you may never get a call at all.

Consistency in your interactions and communications is important to establish trust and comfort. In fact, your actions and words need to always match if you want to make people feel safe, eliminate as much uncertainty as possible, and build trust.

Interactive Uncertainty Reduction

The third, and most direct, of the uncertainty reduction strategies is to have an actual (gasp) conversation. In business today, this typically doesn't happen without some comfort level already having been established. This is where a lot of what you've already read in this book can come into play. To aid yourself and your communication partner(s) in this process, state facts and the information needed to process the idea or make a decision right at the outset. State the purpose for each meeting at the beginning so everyone understands.

To interactively reduce uncertainty, ask:

⊙ Is there any information you would like to know prior to meeting?
⊙ Is there any information I need to prepare to make the meeting more productive?

Basically, you're asking your communicative partner what they need you to do to help them reduce uncertainty about you, your product, your service, and your company. By doing this, you are proactively attempting to establish the community of trust and a dialogue in the conversation. This will make the initial interaction, meaning the first meeting, much more productive and comfortable for both parties.

Now you know all about this theory and some ways to think about it in your business. Let's look at some examples of everyday uncertainty that happen in businesses, communication strategies for avoiding uncertainty, and the potential impacts that not reducing uncertainty can have on your bottom line.

Ambiguous Messages

Ambiguous messages can create unease in employees. "Come to my office when you get a chance." "I'd like to talk to you about this project." While we may think these are straightforward and succinct, they create uncertainty in the minds of employees. How does an employee know if coming to your office is a positive or negative request? If we think back to childhood, being asked to come to the principal's office was typically not a good thing; in fact, it often caused anxiety. Anxiety creates stress, and when people are stressed they find a way to become de-stressed.

This can negatively affect productivity, especially if part of that de-stressing is interrupting the work of others to ask, "What do you think the boss meant by this?" The residual impacts of uncertainty in this scenario are obvious.

SPOILER ALERT

In Chapter 22 we'll look at some important aspects of equity and fairness in the workplace and how communication plays a big role in managing people— especially people who are experiencing stress.

REAL PEOPLE, REAL STORIES, REAL RESULTS

Sylvie di Giusto

CEO and Founder, Executive Image Consulting

Your Image Is Offline and Online

Your appearance, behavior, and communication are all part of your image. But your digital footprint is also a big part. Right now somebody could Google you and make a major decision based on what they find. Paying attention to these ABCD's—appearance, behavior, communication, and digital footprint—are important to your image as an entrepreneur.

Subsequent Impressions Are Affected by Confirmation Bias

Once a first impression is formed, there is a powerful source called confirmation bias that works for or against you. Whatever that impression was—positive or negative— people are going to find things that confirm their initial impression in your appearance and your behavior and everything they see, because we want to be right. We look for proof and ignore everything that speaks against our first initial opinion.

We Make 3,000 Judgments Per Day

We get judged and we judge each other around 3,000 times per day, from the first person we see, to people we pass on the street, to images we see online. We judge and form opinions quickly. Some say it happens in seven seconds, some in three seconds, others in ten seconds. The time really doesn't matter. What matters is that it happens. So we need to make an effort to make a very powerful first impression.

Confidence Is Your Best Designer

You cannot get a better piece of clothing more suitable than confidence. If you walk in a room and if you know who you are, if you're authentic to yourself, and if you show that from the very beginning, you are in the game. A lot of people think it has something to do with fashion, but it's not about fashion. It's about speaking with your appearance, speaking with your body, and being true to your image.

The First 11 Words You Say Are Important

In every single conversation, we have a huge opportunity in the first 11 words. How do you start those conversations? What do you say? Most people waste it with "How are you doing?" Done. You won't be remembered for "How are you doing?" You have another chance with the close. Many people remember you for how you close those conversations, how they feel when you leave them behind.

Defining Your Personal Style and Image

Define your personal style by thinking of one word that you want to be known for— the word that should pop into everybody's mind when they think of you. Then think of the one word that your clients need to know you to be. Often it's not the same. We're all entrepreneurs and we all want to sell a product or service, so we cannot ignore what our clients want to see in us. We have to take our word and their word and fill in the gap.

Don't assume your employees know the context of your request. If you look at the message in isolation, are there multiple ways to interpret the communication? If so, clarify. Look at the message and ask yourself if it could be interpreted in a negative way (assuming that's not your intent). If so, readjust the wording or be more specific. State why the request is being made.

For example, instead of simply saying, "Come to my office when you get a chance," rephrase it to: "Come to my office when you get a chance. I'd like to get your thoughts on a new product."

State the action and the purpose for the action with your communication. Action plus purpose drives awareness. Awareness leads to engagement. Engagement leads to results.

Customer Uncertainty

We've talked about the importance of communication history and how consumers are actively looking for information on you to reduce their uncertainty about contacting you in the first place. We also just saw some examples of messaging in the workplace that can negatively impact productivity when uncertainty is present. Now let's look at an example of customer uncertainty that arises once someone is using your product or service, and the importance of proactive communication.

Have you ever been on a flight that experienced unexpected turbulence? The type of turbulence that causes audible gasps and maybe even some screams? The type that leaves passengers looking around for answers?

If you have, you know what I'm talking about and the questions that immediately pop into your head. If you haven't, you can imagine the fear that some people might experience in that moment. This is just one example of why it is so important for businesses to communicate about any anticipated turbulence points—or bumps in the road.

Whenever possible, the best pilots will proactively communicate about anticipated turbulence: "Ladies and gentlemen, the radar is showing us that we're going to be experiencing a fair amount of turbulence soon, so I'm going to go ahead and turn on the fasten seat belt sign."

And if things don't get much better, following up by telling your customers the action you're going to take can help reduce uncertainty. Or, if your changes are still in process, updating customers on the situation can also help: "Ladies and gentlemen, that was a pretty big gust we just ran into, but there's nothing to worry about. I'm going to drop to a lower elevation to see if we can get under this system."

These messages let us know what's coming, and tell us what will be done to remedy the situation. Business leaders can learn from pilot communication. If a bump in the road is anticipated, communicate about it. If you're going to take corrective action to avoid conflict, let your customers and/or team, know. Not communicating in these situations leaves people in an awkward and uncertain position, forcing them to draw their own conclusions. If you want to make sure they are the right conclusions, proactively communicate.

⊙   ⊙   ⊙

In the next chapter, we'll look at an important, but often ignored, element of dynamic communication: listening. We'll have two chapters on listening. The first is how you listen to others. The second is how others listen to you.

Shut Up and Listen!

Skills for Listening to Others

When I used to teach business communication courses and the chapter on listening would come up, students would often ask, "Why aren't we taught this stuff sooner?" I told them that was a darn good question, but that I was committed to teaching it to them now. Better late than never, right?

I understand their frustration. It's such an important topic! I know many business schools that don't even teach the subject at all. Yet I don't know a business leader who is successful without it.

So consider this chapter and the next the course on listening you may never have had. I'll go into some of the academic jargon, but in a way that you can apply and use to better yourself and those around you.

Hearing vs. Listening

Hearing is the physical act of recognizing sound. Just because you can hear something doesn't mean you're listening. My elementary schoolteacher's voice haunts me to this day: "You aren't listening to me!" she said, before taking away our recess time. And she wasn't wrong. We weren't listening.

Listening takes hearing a step further. Listening is the process of realizing that those sounds you're hearing have meaning. Let's do an experiment.

Go to a public place where there are other people around. Clap your hands once. You just made a sound. Did people look at you? Did they immediately look away? Did anyone ask you why you clapped? (OK, if you're in New York City they might not even look, but in most other places they will.)

The act of clapping your hands makes a sound. The sound is heard by those in the near vicinity with the physical ability to hear. But only if the people around you go beyond recognizing the sound to processing the meaning of why the sound was made will they have listened. If someone came up to ask why you clapped, then that person moved from hearing (recognizing the sound) to listening (processing the meaning of the sound).

Hearing is a physical process. Listening is a mental process. You can have the most beautifully crafted, well-written, exquisitely organized message in the world. But if nobody is listening, it's moot. Got it? Good. Now let's dive into why this information is important to communication and how it can ultimately impact your bottom line.

What You Need to Know About Active Listening

Now that the difference between hearing and listening is clear, it's time to dive into the meat and potatoes (or tofu and potatoes, if you prefer) of this chapter—understanding what you need to know beyond hearing so that you can use listening to grow your business and better lead and manage your teams.

You've likely heard the phrase "active listening" before. Sometimes it's used interchangeably with "reflective listening." I won't get into the semantics of one vs. the other, but here's what's important to know.

In the 1980s two researchers, William Newkirk and Richard Linden, studied communication between emergency medical services

(EMS) and patients. After many observations and experimental situations, what resulted was the need for a listening strategy that would ensure that the patient was not only heard, but also understood, so the best care could be provided as quickly as possible. And, voilà, active listening was born.

With active listening, you listen to someone and then repeat what you comprehended in your own words back to them. Essentially, you're paraphrasing. The idea is that you create mutual understanding so that there are no ambiguities in interpretation. This concept of mutual understanding is central for driving action in many communication strategies, and this isn't the last time you'll hear the phrase in this book.

Active listening is more than posturing your body toward a person and showing nonverbal signs that you're paying attention, such as nodding your head. While these nonverbal signs are important, the true magic of active listening lies in your ability to understand the conversation from the perspective of your communication partner and your willingness to genuinely invest time in listening to their full story.

This means that you listen without formulating your response.

We've all done it, especially in conflict or debate situations where you're ready to fire back. But that's not healthy, and it's not productive. Doing that in the workplace will demoralize those around you, make you less of a team player, and position you as more of a narcissist than I'm guessing you want to appear.

Mirroring Is Not Active Listening

Let me be clear—mirroring is not active listening. Rather, mirroring is a strategy where behaviors are reflected between communication partners. With mirroring, one person—often subconsciously—mirrors the behaviors, actions and words; the rate of speech; and the pitch of another. The goal of mirroring is to establish rapport, to match your conversational partner, and to build a connection. But if you do this too obviously, it can come off as mocking. The best mirroring is subtle.

For example, when one person raises his voice, the other is more likely to follow—to mirror that behavior. Or have you ever been in a relationship where, after a while, you start noticing that you're using

REAL PEOPLE, REAL STORIES, REAL RESULTS

Noah Fleming

CEO and Founder, Fleming Consulting and Co.

If You Ask for Feedback, You Have to Take Action on It

The simplest and most effective way to appreciate your customers is to show them that you're actually listening and paying attention. If you reach out to a customer for feedback, you need to read and take action on the feedback—and communicate that action to your customers. I know a lot of companies that collect feedback. They survey their customers and look for the aggregate point score, but they don't really do anything with the data. You have to use that feedback to actually create some meaningful change.

Customer Loyalty Is Never Owed

No matter how loyal you think your customers are, they're really only loyal up until that last transaction, or up until the last time you speak to them. That's why there's so much connection between sales, marketing, and customer service. They all really gel together, because loyalty is a function of day-in-and-day-out marketing, being front-facing with your customers, and being there when they're looking to get that next piece of work done.

Focus on Evergreen Clients—Keeping the Clients You Have

The problem with the chase is that it's done at the expense of recurring customers. You have current customers that have already said, "I've raised my hands. I'm willing to do business with you," but meanwhile, your salespeople have already gone on to working on the next big thing. If you only ever hear your sales and marketing team talking about the next great promotion, or their next great lead, or next great opportunity, then they're really only doing half their jobs.

Customer Disengagement Is Often the Result of a Simple Behavior Change

Any change with a customer is almost always a simple behavior change. If you've got a web business, the simple behavior change is somebody stops logging in. If you have a traditional retail business, you have to know what the buying cycle is. If a customer misses the typical buying window, that's a behavior change.

One of my favorite examples of this is an online subscription site where they were doing a few million dollars a month in revenue. They would get tons of new signups, but one demographic kept dropping off. About two weeks into signing up, they would lose these customers. In fact, not only would they lose them, they would get chargebacks on their credit cards and fraud complaints. Finally, somebody asked a very simple question: "What's going on with these people? Let's reach out and see what's actually happening." It turned out that the majority of these people didn't know how to retrieve a lost password, and they assumed that they had been scammed. The issue was solved by making one simple change.

You can apply the same logic to any business, offline, online, and anything in between. You can look for those simple key performance indicators, that the things you expect to be happening are actually happening.

---

some of the phrases that your partner often uses, and vice versa? This is subconscious mirroring. And note that mirroring is not mimicking.

I once took a workshop on listening and note-taking. In that hour, we were taught to take notes and circle words that appeared more than once, and to make sure we mirrored or repeated those words back in the conversation to try and get sales. That would make us a good listener.

While I liked the circling strategy for taking notes, I strongly disagreed that it made me a good listener. It demonstrated I was capable of repeating things back. But I'd like to think I'm more than a parrot. (In fact, in communication, parroting is a term used to describe repeating something back word-for-word!)

Strategies for Being a Better Listener

I've subtly dropped most of these in already, but I'm going to present them to you in a rapid-fire format so no meaning is lost. If you're ready to become a better listener, do these things:

Check Your Ego—you cannot truly listen if you're more worried about your own personal outcome in a conversation than creating a positive outcome for all involved.

Stop Thinking About Your Response—if you're formulating your response in your head while the other person is speaking, you're not listening!

Acknowledge Feelings—when listening, you don't always have to agree with what the other person says or feels, but good listeners and strong communicators acknowledge that those feelings were heard.

Nonverbally Show Engagement—a slight tilt of the head, a forward lean of the body, head nods, small "uh-huh" utterances, maintaining eye contact . . . all these things encourage engagement in a conversation and are indicators of listening.

Admit When You Didn't Listen—or at least ask someone to repeat themselves. "I didn't quite catch that. Could you please repeat?" It's better to have the full picture in a conversation than to make a judgment call or decision on something without all the puzzle pieces in play.

Use Active Listening—make sure you heard what the person intended. So many conflicts could be avoided in the workplace and so many teams would run more smoothly if people would just check for mutual understanding. Do it. You'll see a difference in the productivity, the relationships, and the outcomes.

⊙　⊙　⊙

In the next chapter, now that you know strategies for effectively listening to others, we'll tackle the other side of listening—how to know how others are listening to you. This is especially useful for sales conversations, or any conversations where you're trying to drive people to act.

Sales Machine/ Ninja/Badass

Providing Service and Growing Sales

The Listening Matrix

Sell More by Knowing How Others Listen to You

In the previous chapter, we talked about how you listen to others. In this chapter, we take that knowledge a bit further and learn how to communicate more dynamically in sales conversations by understanding how your potential customer is listening to *you*.

I'm not worried as much about how you're listening to them. I'm hoping that as a businessperson, and as someone who read the previous chapter, you understand how to do that by now. In order to move people to action, you need to understand how people are listening to you. You're flipping the listening paradigm on its head and approaching it from the opposite perspective.

How are they listening to you? Are they listening for information, or are they listening for knowledge? The answer is the difference between action and inaction—making a sale or missing an opportunity.

How someone understands the information being presented and how relevant a specific piece of information is to them are determining factors in how they listen. This is true for every person you meet, every encounter you have, every conversation you start, and every message you send.

From the moment you enter into a communicative episode, your audience (whether an audience of one or an audience of millions) is determining if they want to be listening for information or for knowledge. The difference is huge.

When people are listening for information, they aren't going to make an action or purchase decision. At best they're going to decide that they need to learn more. At worst, you lose an opportunity. In order to move your audience to action, you must get them to listen for knowledge and engage in a conversation at that level.

REAL PEOPLE, REAL STORIES, REAL RESULTS

Grant Cardone

CEO and Founder, Cardone Enterprises, *New York Times* Bestselling Author

You Can Never Stop Selling

Any time you're launching something, no matter how successful you are, you still have to put effort into selling it. Most people put all the emphasis on creating, but you actually have to put emphasis and effort on selling the thing. Otherwise, the idea, the feeling, the inspiration, whatever it is you have in your product is never going to get transferred to another human being. Get it to market, push it, keep pushing it, push it long after everybody says you're pushing too hard.

If Someone Tells You "You're Promoting Too Much," They're Really Saying It to Themselves

You need to understand that when you're told, "Don't promote. Don't market," that you need to promote and market more. They're telling you you're in the neighborhood, you have entered the ZIP code of success. The hater is telling you you're getting close. Use it as a signpost saying, "Oh, this is go. Accelerate."

You Cannot Be Successful Without Haters

You don't need to stop the hater. You don't need to confront them. You don't need to talk to them. You don't even need to block them. Use them. You cannot be successful without haters. It will not happen. Success is not a popularity contest. If you're going to be the quarterback, if you're going to be the head cheerleader, if you're going to be Miss Universe, if you're going to be the president, you're going to get some hate.

Make the Perfect Pitch for Your Customer, Not for You

When I started out I would go to a customer, knock on a door cold, and say, "Hey, look, man. Give me three minutes. I've got something I want to tell you. I can help your business." The problem was, in the vertical that I had focused on, they were already making a lot of money. They had a problem they weren't aware of, but what I didn't calculate was that they were already happy making the money they were making. I couldn't even get their attention. My pitch was so wrong. I thought it was perfect, but it was perfect for me, not perfect for them.

When Your Pitch Doesn't Work, Take Responsibility

If your sales pitch doesn't work, don't blame anyone else. That's not going to make things better. Even if your customer is cheap, don't blame the customer. Take responsibility for it. They're not paying you enough money because of something you're doing. When my first business didn't work right away, I basically wrote down everything they told me. I assumed that I was the reason, not them. I didn't blame the economy, or the market, or the competitor. I said, "OK. It's something I'm doing." Take responsibility, and don't quit. Be obsessed with figuring it out.

Your goal in the sales conversation is to ask the right questions. Most people go into any type of sales conversation thinking they need to give information, give information, give information. No. Go in and ask the right questions. That will help you ascertain how to transition them from information to knowledge faster. So how do you make that transition? Enter the listening matrix.

4 / The Listening Matrix

The Listening Matrix

The listening matrix is a four-stage continuum for understanding how someone is listening to you. The further you progress along the continuum, the more likely you are to be able to drive your audience to action or facilitate buy-in.

Depending on which stage your audience is in, you'll use different communication strategies, including questions and messages, to move your audience closer to a decision. People who listen for information do not decide. People who listen for knowledge decide. That's the dichotomy. We want them to decide.

Everything in business comes down to decisions. If you don't have a decision, you're floating on a plateau. Lack of decision means a lack of, or leaking, profit.

The matrix has four parts, or stages (Figure 4-1). On the left side are the two stages of listening for information. On the right side are the two stages of listening for knowledge. Let's examine each stage in more detail and learn how to drive conversations that lead to knowledge and well-informed decisions.

Stage One: The Writer

You're talking, their hand is quickly writing. At this point the audience is listening to you, but you can't tell if they are truly engaged. If

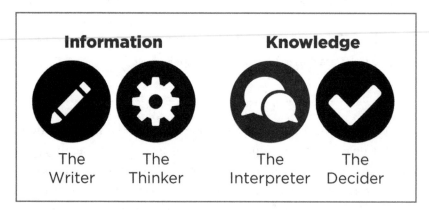

FIGURE 4–1
The Listening Matrix

someone is listening to you as a writer, they are listening to take notes, get general information, and perhaps relay this information to someone else. Or because that's what they do out of habit. Or, perhaps, they're taking notes to be polite and look interested. No matter how you slice it, you must progress past this stage if you want them to take action. You must turn the writer into a thinker.

The writer is not making a decision. The writer is there to collect information. This is often a person that's sent on behalf of someone else to retrieve information—almost like a reconnaissance mission.

In this stage, no decision whatsoever is going to be made. If you're in a meeting with a potential client and all they're doing is sitting there taking notes, in order for them to make a decision, you're eventually going to have to get them to put that pen down and then pick it back up to sign on the dotted line.

Unfortunately, this is one of the more difficult transitions to make, especially in the United States, as our habits of listening are deeply rooted and perpetuated in an educational system where you listen for information so you can achieve a high score on a standardized, multiple-choice test.

Though difficult, have no fear. Transitioning your audience from a writer to a thinker can be done. And it can be done with a relatively simple line of questioning:

- ⊙ What do you think about [insert topic]?
- ⊙ What is your opinion on [insert topic]?
- ⊙ What are your feelings on [insert topic]?
- ⊙ What is your view on [insert topic]?
- ⊙ What is your perspective on [insert topic]?

A popular saying in organizational development states that people support what they help create. By asking these questions, you're inviting your audience to co-create meaning with you, to engage in dialogue about a product, service, idea, or decision.

As human beings, we like to know that our opinions and thoughts matter. We like to know that we are a part of something bigger than ourselves. Asking your audience to stop writing and start thinking will get them to start identifying with the information that you're providing on a personal level. This is a precursor to getting them to place the information in a bigger, decision-driving context.

Using these questions, it's possible that you'll skip over stage two (the thinker) completely and transition right into stage three (the interpreter). You'll know if that's the case because their answers will start coinciding with the bigger picture for your communication—how the topic you're discussing helps their business at a broader level.

> **SPOILER ALERT**
>
> We'll talk more about communicating for buy-in, co-creating meaning, and really fostering a "people support what they help create" mentality with your communication in Chapter 21.

For example, if you're pitching a product or service, they'll start asking about how it fits into a context or serves a need. But if they're not there yet, and they're still listening for information, that's OK. We've moved them into the next stage. Either way, you're making progress.

Stage Two: The Thinker

Either you've gotten your audience engaged at a thinking level or they researched you a lot ahead of time and started out in this stage. Either way, you're still stuck in information purgatory, and your goal is to advance your listener into the knowledge side of the matrix.

At this stage your audience is still listening for information, but they may ask questions to clarify facts, figures, features, details, etc. When they step back from their notes for a second to begin to process, that means that the decision-making engine is starting and they are likely at a pivotal point, where they're deciding if the information is worth investing more energy in, thus moving their listening into the knowledge camp.

Either way, you need to get your audience listening at a deeper level. Here are a few questions to help guide your conversation in this stage.

⊙ What do you know about [insert subject]?

⊙ Would you share with me what you know about [insert subject]?

⊙ What does your company know about [insert subject]?

With these questions, you're figuring out what your audience knows, or what their company knows, and you're getting them to start thinking in a bigger context. Once they're thinking at this level, it's easy to transition them to the knowledge side if what you're presenting is a good fit and you have a connection established.

For someone who comes in having done a lot of research, you're asking your potential client, who already thinks she knows a lot, to share what she knows with you. You're in fact asking her to demonstrate her awesomeness. Who doesn't like to do that? But, in reality, you're checking to see what information she has at her disposal: what reports she's consumed, what commercials she's seen, and what conversations she's had. This is incredibly valuable intelligence to have when you're trying to move someone to action. It also allows you to know what misinformation they have, so you know what context or perspective you need to provide to move into the true knowledge portion of the continuum.

With this line of questioning, it's possible to significantly expedite the decision-making process. If the information your audience has is accurate and favorable, it's easier to place it into an organizational context and proceed with your request. And if you need an extra push, here's a question that has saved many a conversation and helped lead to more action (especially closed sales): How do you see that process working for your business? Note that this is not a yes/no, closed question. It's a question that generates further discussion.

Now we're getting people to think of how they will apply the solution you're offering in their business for positive gain. And if you get them to

FLASHBACK

Remember how we discussed communication history in Chapter 1? That comes into play heavily in the information side of the matrix. Don't you like how this is all starting to fit together?

engage in this conversation, now they're listening for knowledge. Let's look at the other side of the matrix.

Stage Three: The Interpreter

If your connection is strong and your communication is on point, you've earned your audience's attention at a knowledge level. Bravo!

The interpreter stage is when your audience starts to interpret how something will apply—its consequences, its benefits—in their business.

Now that you're on the knowledge half of the matrix, you're closer to having your audience take action. At the interpreter stage, your audience has decided that they want to know more—and not just information. They want to know how the information you're providing will look in their context. You'll know you're in this stage when they start asking questions about how something you presented applies in their world, at their company, in their home, etc.

Often in this stage, you're not asking many of the questions. Your audience is. However, if you're not quite there yet, here are a few questions that can help you make the transition. Focus on the benefits that your idea, product, service, etc. will bring to the table. Get your audience to show that they're adapting your information to their context. Remember, knowledge is information applied.

- ☉ How would your business change if . . . ?
- ☉ What would it look like if your organization used . . . ?
- ☉ How would your job be easier if . . . ?
- ☉ What would be the best outcome for you if . . . ?
- ☉ How would you react if . . . ?
- ☉ What would it take for this to work in your . . . ?

With these questions your audience is interpreting how this information makes sense in their world. You want people to be in this stage, because this is where you really prove your expertise. It's a brilliant part.

By getting answers to these questions, you'll be able to understand where your audience's mind is positioned relative to your topic. You'll also be able to ascertain how others see your idea, product, or service in their world. This is valuable not only for the present conversation, but also for future communicative episodes with this or other audiences.

When you know how others are applying the information at their disposal, you're armed with useful intel.

If you're pitching a product or service, your audience is placing it into a context for you. This is a big gift in sales. As a bonus, you know whether your product can help in other areas of the business. If it can, verbally agree with your audience about their idea(s) for implementation and then add in what else your solution may provide. It's the icing on the cake.

When you've gotten your audience to listen at this level, you're truly engaging in dialogue. Now it's time to take this discussion to the next level and move your audience to action. Your goal is to get to a decision phase—whatever that decision may be. Let's get to the decider.

Stage Four: The Decider

It's now or never. It's do or die. It's . . . well, it's not really that polarizing, but it's time to get your audience to make a commitment to act. And if your audience is listening in this stage, they're primed to make some type of decision. The deciders are ready to go.

Your success in this stage will be determined on how well you've connected with your audience and how well you articulate your request. If you reach this stage of listening, unless there is a fundamental shortcoming of some sort (such as your product not meeting a necessary requirement), you've formed a relationship that, if it doesn't bear fruit at this point in the conversation, will likely produce in the future.

Your job in this stage is to get the action. That means you want to hear them say "yes" to the majority of questions you ask and ultimately to your final ask—to sign on that dotted line (or the equivalent). Here are a few sample questions you can adapt to your situation and use to make sure you're driving this conversation toward the finish line.

☉ Can you see this working for your business?
☉ Do you see this meeting your needs?

- ⊙ Are you comfortable recommending this to your board?
- ⊙ Is this solution within your budget?
- ⊙ Do you want to get started today?
- ⊙ Is this something you feel your sales team could benefit from?
- ⊙ Shall we talk about some solutions that we can work on together?
- ⊙ Your business is the type of business I love to serve. I would be honored to work with you if you feel it's the right fit. Do you want to have that conversation now?

No matter what, at this stage you need to get a "yes" or "no" and move to the next step of the relationship. The "yes" could be to a future conversation, an on-site demo, a meeting with the CEO, a signed contract, a partnership or merger, or simply an agreed follow-up date. But you have to get a decision—an action—from the conversation, or you'll remain on that previously mentioned plateau.

⊙ ⊙ ⊙

In the next chapter, we'll look at sales scripts and how they can be the downfall of many businesses if they don't leave room for flexibility. As you read the next chapter, keep in mind the previous strategies, especially those about communication history and uncertainty. There'll be plenty of ways to apply the listening techniques, too.

Death by Sales Script

Using Outlines to Create Sales Conversations

After reading Chapter 4, you now know how important it is to pay attention to how others are listening to you. By doing this, you can adapt the questions you ask to their immediate state of mind, addressing their information or knowledge needs and ultimately leading the conversation to a place where they can make a decision.

You also learned that sales conversations are not always linear—that people can go from information to knowledge listening phases at various points during a conversation.

Because of the need to adapt at multiple points in a conversation, it's probably obvious that sales scripts are not always the way to go.

Don't get me wrong: Sales scripts do enable a general flow of information, an organized presentation of material, and a conversational guideline from which new salespeople can springboard. The script itself isn't the problem. The problem arises when the company expects a salesperson to adhere strictly to the script. This is why I call this chapter death by sales script.

There are, however, some generalized tendencies that we as human beings have. Understanding these, and being willing to let your salespeople adapt their scripts as they see fit, can lead to positive results.

A Universal Script for Human Interaction Doesn't Exist

People want to be treated as individuals. This is true of your employees, the general public, and your customers and potential customers. Using a sales script to craft a conversation is a misnomer. If you're using a script, you're not actually having a conversation because there really is no back-and-forth, just one prescribed line after another.

At best, a sales script moves you to the next stage in the sales life cycle. At worst, you completely alienate a potential customer. What happens in many cases, though, is that you confuse the customer or waste his time. If sales were a scripted process, we wouldn't need salespeople. Instead we could have sales machines. But humans are not robots, and when you treat them as such you don't get anywhere.

Even though technology (bots, auto-responders, and the like) has come a long way, it's still not there quite yet. Think of how frustrating it is when trying to reach a customer service representative and the voice-recognition technology doesn't work, or you're sent down a labyrinth of options until you can actually request to speak to a human (I know I've screamed a few choice words on those phone calls before).

Most sales scripts are incredibly impersonal. And when a script is strictly adhered to, you lack the human touch and personal connection that lead to a sale. It also tells me that, as a potential customer, the person I'm speaking with likely doesn't have the knowledge I need to make a product or service work for me and my business.

When somebody's communication style is not adaptable, and it's obvious that they're sticking to a pre-written script, it's clear that my needs, questions, and wants are not being truly taken

FLASHBACK

In Chapter 4 there are a number of questions you can use to make sure the real wants and needs of your customer are communicated.

into consideration. It's more like a sales interrogation than a sales conversation. People don't buy when they are being interrogated.

REAL PEOPLE, REAL STORIES, REAL RESULTS

Lisa Sasevich

CEO and Founder, The Invisible Close

To Convert, Set Aside the Canned Scripts

This idea of sales conversion is really about putting aside what you're talking about—the scripts and the canned lines. Instead, really think about what kind of invitation you can make that would be irresistible to your ideal prospective clients, the people who when they hear your invitation—or your irresistible offer—would thank you for it. To do that, you must put aside anything rote or scripted.

Be Committed, But Not Attached

When you structure your offer right, your audience should be able to know right away if it's a fit. We call the idea that a sales conversation needs to get someone to a decision "committed, but not attached." You're committed with the knowledge that your prospective client has what they need to make a decision, but you're not attached to which decision they make, yes or no.

Not Making an Offer Is a Disservice

When it comes to sales, one of the biggest mistakes is not asking. It's not making the offer. We get out there and we inspire. It's like we roll people out into this lake of possibility of what could happen in their life, and if we don't make the offer, if we don't make that invitation, I really think it's a disservice. It's like taking them out in this lake of possibility and then leaving them with no oars.

Figure Out the Unique Transformation You Offer

Think of one client you've helped, the one client you'd really like 100 or 1,000 of. Answer these questions thinking only of this client:

1. What are the exact results this person had?

2. What are the additional transformations that happened to this client through working with you?

3. What would the costs to this person have been if he had not accepted your offer?

By doing this, you'll end up with all kinds of words you can pull together to communicate about the unique transformation you have to offer.

Communicate Your Offer in Their Words

To make an offer, you need to have confidence and your communication needs to exude that. Show confidence so your audience knows that your offer is something proven and a process they can trust. Communicate your offer in their words, words they can relate to, and show them there's a method to your madness—that you have a system that is unique and gets the job done. And then the big one: Be able to make that offer in a way they can't turn down. Make an irresistible offer.

The Sales Call Outline

Instead of a sales script, use a sales outline. For each point of the outline, state the intention of that segment and what you want the salesperson to accomplish. Then you can provide an example for those who are just starting out. Here's a sample table you can adapt for your business for basic outbound sales calls (see Figure 5–1 on page 41).

If you aren't already convinced that the sales outline is the way to go, let me break down an actual telesales script for you—it accomplishes the same task as the outline, but in a very different way.

Hello, [prospect], this is [name] calling from [business name]. Have I caught you in the middle of anything?

I hate this question. Of course you caught them in the middle of something. Any time you're changing the status quo, you're stopping something and starting something else.

The purpose for my call is that we help businesses improve the performance of their business-critical applications.

Part of Call	What You Need to Accomplish	Example of How to Say It
Introduction	• Introduce yourself. • Introduce business. • State connection or referral.	Hi, (*prospect*). This is (*name*) calling from (*business*). • We met at (*connection event*). • (*Referring*) gave me your name. • I'm also a member of (*connection organization*).
Purpose	• State reason for call. • Relate to person.	I'm calling to talk about (*state reason*). (*Then find a connection or relation.*) • It's a new process that many others in the (*industry*) field are using. • (*Referring*) mentioned you were looking for a solution. • Other members in (*organization*) have found success with . . .
Qualify	• Find out if you're talking to a decision-maker.	(*If you already know, you can skip this part.*) • Are you the person who chooses what (*product*) solutions your business uses?

FIGURE 5–1

Breakdown of a Sales Call

5 / Death by Sales Script

Part of Call	What You Need to Accomplish	Example of How to Say It
Ask	• Ask for decision-maker. • Make request. • Confirm and personalize.	(*If the answer to the previous question is no . . .*) • Do you know who is? • Would you mind connecting us? • Could you provide her contact information? (*If the answer to the previous question is yes . . .*) May we set up a time to do a product demo next week? Great! Our (*position*), (*name*), will do that demo with you on (*date*) at (*time, location*).

FIGURE 5–1

Breakdown of a Sales Call, continued

What this does is immediately puts your prospect into the "do I need this" or "why are you calling me" mindset. Neither is great.

I actually do not know if you need what we provide, and this is why I have a couple of questions. [Insert questions.]

This is in the pushing information mentality instead of pulling. You're trying to see if what you have is a fit, which isn't inherently bad, but you're missing the opportunity to find out if the potential customer needs something else that you could provide. And even if you couldn't provide that service but could provide value in some other way (such as a referral to a partner provider), you would still be useful and make a favorable impression.

Are you available to put a brief 15- to 20-minute meeting on the calendar where we can discuss this in more detail and share any insight and value that we have to offer?

First, if some value isn't already inherent, or you're not offering something of value, this ask is premature. Nobody likes a premature ask-escalation. Second, this is an awfully long sentence. Third, it's still about pushing—you want to tell them what you have to offer.

A major part of the issue is that sales scripts tend to focus on information and features rather than benefits or applied applications and knowledge.

The script outline provided on the previous pages is used for an initial conversation. Let's take a look at another type of sales conversation where a script is often used—the sales demonstration.

The Sales Demonstration

You've gotten past the initial conversation, and now it's time to demonstrate what your product can do. In many demonstrations, it's typical to go through the features of the product. There is usually a script or outline for this. And in my experience, most salespeople will stick to this script instead of asking questions to help them discover the needs of the customer and tailor the demonstration to that.

When this happens, it can also be indicative of a larger, systemic problem, where salespeople in a company really don't know or understand the product and its application to the customer's world. If your sales teams can't provide use-case scenarios or adapt the product to a specific situation, you may want to rethink your training strategy.

This was evident when I was on a product demo for a business CRM software solution. After doing my research, I filled out the contact form on the company's website, stating specifically what parts of the product I was interested in, what my budget was, and two questions I had. When I got on the virtual demonstration, the salesperson stuck to a script, listing off the features and going piece by piece through different aspects of the software. He didn't mention anything about the notes I submitted ahead of time, nor did he acknowledge my questions. After interrupting three times, I finally got the answers to the two questions I had asked. My time was wasted, I was frustrated, and the salesperson listed a bunch of features I really didn't care about—nor were they in my budget at the time. Even though the product would have fit my needs, I chose not to work with the company and went with another (more expensive) provider simply because the salesperson did not pay attention to my needs.

And I'm not the only one making decisions like this. In a society where your product can easily be substituted for another, your service and the customer experience are what will attract and retain clients.

Another reason sales scripts or outlines used in demos tend to be problematic is that they often use the features and jargon native to a product, instead of explaining it in a way that is more universal. Let me tell you how this could have cost one of my clients a large contract.

I was in a sales meeting with a learning management software company that was trying to get the business of a large national association. My role was to evaluate the communication from both sides and see where there were missed opportunities. After a somewhat tedious back and forth, it became clear to me that the salesperson was communicating in the jargon native to their product, whereas the potential client was communicating using vocabulary that reflected their basic understanding of online learning.

Even though the two parties were talking about the same thing, neither of them knew it because they were so wrapped up in their own individual understandings. The product sales scripts were evident, as the salesperson was relying heavily on the features of their system instead of addressing the broader needs of the client in their own terminology.

As I was hired to do, I interjected and explained that what one party was calling a module, the other was referring to as a content silo. Both parties were talking about the same thing, but in completely different language. That simple comment changed the trajectory of the conversation, and we were able to move the discussion forward to the contract stage.

When it comes to sales demonstrations, think of providing conversation guides instead of scripts. By doing this, you are empowering your employees to better address the needs of the customer. This guide should contain all the product features, but also columns with synonyms, benefits, and value propositions. Figure 5–2 is a sample you can use for your business.

Finally, to help with your sales demonstration guides, ask your support team or your sales staff what the most frequently asked

Feature	Synonyms	Benefits	Value
Name of the product feature (e.g., data sorting, two-hour webinar, coaching access, wrinkle-resistant fabric)	Words often used by others to explain this feature, analogies, and metaphors used to explain this feature to people not familiar with your type of product	What benefits does this feature provide? What does this feature help someone do?	State the value of this feature. Think of your value proposition. This is about the end result, the experience, and the feeling.

FIGURE 5–2

Conversation Guides

questions are during sales demos. If you don't already document this, start doing so. This will alert you to some of the features or jargon you use that might be confusing to your customers. This is ridiculously valuable information that can help you create better conversations in the future.

⊙ ⊙ ⊙

In the next chapter, we'll expand upon addressing the needs of the consumer and providing an experience that attracts and retains your clients. It's a new concept that is motivated and inspired by an old design, and I'm excited to share it with you.

Be Open 24/7

Panopticon-Style Service

In today's digital world, there's no such thing as business hours. A business can never truly be "closed" anymore. That's not to say that your physical office space doesn't shut down, but your customers, and your potential customers, expect access to you 24/7. Whether that comes in the form of locating information on your website, engagement and interaction on and with your social media channels, or leaving a review on a third-party site, your business is always "open." You can never stop paying attention.

Enter the Panopticon.

The what?!

The Pan-op-ti-con. Let me put on my professor hat and explain.

It was the late 18th century, and this English philosopher, Jeremy Bentham, was hanging with his brother Samuel in what is now known as Belarus. Samuel was working on industrial projects for some royal figure, and Jeremy came to visit. They probably had a vodka shot or two, and Samuel began musing about a design that would allow a manager to easily observe his whole workforce. The idea was to make a round building with another, smaller round building in the middle of it. From the smaller building, managers could oversee all the employees at once. (I like to think they built a model with empty shot glasses when conceptualizing this design.)

Jeremy then took that idea and said, "Hmmm . . . I think it's quite good. Let's see how it can be applied in prisons." Because that would be anyone's first thought. Clearly. It turns out Jeremy was on to something, because the idea of inmates being observed from a centralized tower started to catch on. And as the design was adapted and altered, it began to be designed so that the guards could see out, but the prisoners couldn't see in. So they never really knew if they were being watched or not. This made the inmates behave better, because the possibility of being monitored all the time was threat enough to keep them in line. And the implementation of the Panopticon design spread.

WTF Does This Have to Do with Customer Service?

Now why on earth am I talking about a prison surveillance system in a communication strategy book? Well, because your customers want to know that you are there for them 24/7. They want to feel safe and reassured when they purchase your product that you're always there watching over them. While it's easy to think of the Panopticon in a negative light—it was a prison design, after all—we can flip that around and see how, using this philosophy of constant monitoring with minimal effort thanks to smart design, we can provide better service to our customers.

When your customers believe you are always there for them, and you *are* there for them consistently, they are more likely to trust you and come forward with questions when they have them. *You want your customers to ask questions.*

Questions are a sign that they're actively using or attempting to use your product or service. This type of engagement is indicative of a strong client relationship. Your job as a business owner, then, is to provide the best possible support solutions to your customers based on their needs. With the technology available today, it is easier than ever to create a Panopticon style of service in your organization. The appearance of 24/7 availability communicates to your customers that they are your number-one priority. Of course, this can also apply to your internal audience, as you provide this type of service and support to your employees as well.

Here are some tenets of Panopticon-style service.

The Ability to Communicate at All Times

Offering your customers open communication channels with you and your company at all hours is important. This means having a current web presence with easily accessible contact information, a support team, and a support system (if applicable).

If customers are using your product, they should be able to ask for and get help, no matter what time of day it is. Even if it's only an automated response that tells them your service and support hours, and providing links to possible interim solutions, that's better than leaving them in the dark, not knowing when they'll receive a response. For websites that have live chat features, the best ones let users know where they are in the support queue and how much wait time to anticipate. That's how you show your customer you're there, you realize they have a need, and you're going to address it as soon as possible.

If nothing else, the perception of this availability is essential, especially if you want to reach a global audience (and you need to be cognizant of time zones in your service hours). This perception of being available any time and any place makes an organization seem bigger than it is, communicates a genuine caring for the consumer, and enables open channels of communication where you can get valuable information and feedback.

Providing Comfort and Security to the Customer

Panopticon-style service provides a comfort to the customer, who feels they are being watched over and protected. A failure to provide this communication can increase the likelihood of triggering buyer's remorse (which actually stems from cognitive dissonance . . . uh-oh—the professor hat is going back on).

Maybe you've heard the term "cognitive dissonance," and maybe you've vaguely nodded in recognition, not wanting to ask someone to explain it. So let me clarify it for you so *you* can be the rock star that follows up on those comments with knowledgeable insights in the future.

In the mid-1950s, there was a lot of groundbreaking psychological research being done. And a man named Leon Festinger published a theory in 1957 that is now one of the more widely cited theories when it comes to decision making (and, more important, what happens after the decision is made). This is cognitive dissonance theory.

Long story short, Festinger wanted to understand how people in a cult reacted after the flood they believed would come and destroy the earth, well, didn't happen. Clearly there's a distance between the belief and the reality. Those who were only moderately invested in the cult chalked it up to a learning experience. Those who were heavily involved chose to believe that the earth wasn't destroyed because of the loyalty the cult members demonstrated, reinforcing their faith. This is dissonance. And it's uncomfortable. Think about when you were positive that you were going to get a certain toy for your birthday and then when you opened your presents it wasn't there. Your mind will try to ease that discomfort by making justifications or rationales for why what you believed didn't happen. You try to reduce the dissonance.

When it comes to making decisions, especially ones involving money, you've probably heard terms such as buyer's remorse or post-decision remorse (or, if you're super into studying this, post-purchase cognitive dissonance). Remorse occurs when some sort of cognitive dissonance is in play. And when we start to regret a decision, we start to search for any and all information that will make us not regret said decision. That's where your post-purchase communication is essential. Now that we're all on the same page about this dissonance stuff, let's get back to providing comfort and security and figure out how we can make sure our buyers don't experience any post-decision remorse.

When you put a lot of time and money into a decision, you want to be sure you made the right choice. Customers want to know that the purchase can immediately solve a problem, impact their life in a positive way, or help eliminate something causing them pain or fear. Especially if your product or service is not one of immediate benefit (think instant gratification, like drinking a stellar latte from a local coffee shop on a brisk fall day), providing Panopticon-style service through your communication to your customer post-purchase is essential.

In fact, the communication that comes after the purchase will either confirm or deny the belief that the decision was the right one. If you don't want your customers experiencing remorse or dissonance, you need to find a way to reassure them that their purchase was the right decision, and a good idea. For example, an immediate post-purchase email congratulating them, thanking them, and/or welcoming them to a community. We'll talk more about this in the next section.

REAL PEOPLE, REAL STORIES, REAL RESULTS

Eric Yuan

CEO and Founder, Zoom

Create a Customer-Centric Culture

Our culture is to deliver happiness to our customers. If we cannot make our customer happy, I think nothing else will matter. That's the foundation of our business. Our goal is not only to make sure the customer is happy, but also to deliver the "wow" experience—the surprise happiness that comes in the forms of features, quality, support, and price.

Have a Straightforward Value and Communicate It Everywhere

Our value is very straightforward, and just one word: care. We've got to care about our company, our customers, our teammates, and ourselves. This is central to decisions that we make as a company, and we empower employees by sharing this value with them.

Structure Your Business Around the Customer

From the very beginning, we structured the business around the customer. We created a customer department that is kept in the loop with the other [support, marketing, sales, and engineering] departments. We want to make sure that every department, no matter what the role is, thinks about their job from the customer—the end user—perspective instead of a Zoom perspective.

Decrease the Distance from User to Developer

We intentionally do not have project managers for our engineering and development teams. Between the users and the engineers, you typically have a product manager or a bridge between the end user and the engineers, filtering what gets across. By eliminating that bridge, we make sure that any feedback from customers—good or bad—goes directly to the engineers so they are getting a firsthand account of how customers are using our product. That dramatically makes our internal processes more effective and enables us to create better solutions.

Share How and Why Decisions Are Made

When all employees are interacting with or making decisions that impact customers, we need to make sure we openly communicate why decisions are made, especially when it comes to our support teams, because we want to make sure they take a step back, really talk with the customer, and really understand their problems. And when providing a solution, understanding why a product is designed in a certain way can be very useful.

There's No Secret Sauce for Communicating

Communicating initiatives effectively to employees is a challenge. You can't assume your employees immediately understand what you're talking about the first time you deliver a message, no matter how hard you try. For important initiatives, you've got to talk about it many, many times, across many different channels, until it's ingrained—until it's a part of their DNA. Communicate about it in emails, in all-house meetings, through chat, through video, through everything, especially when it's about your culture.

Multiple Post-Purchase Touch Points

After making a purchase, customers are more likely to engage with you—five times more likely, in fact—within 90 days from the purchase. This means you need to take control of your client onboarding process and provide multiple communication touch points and proactive offers of support. Especially for online purchases or high-value or high-dollar purchases, this type of comfort is essential to avoid purchase regret. You often see great examples of this Panopticon-style service and comfort from ecommerce merchants: they quickly follow up with a thank-you email and direct links to support and contact information.

> **SPOILER ALERT**
>
> One great way to help with client onboarding is to provide a video education campaign and support webinars. We cover these in Chapters 7 and 8.

Create a template or a checklist for this type of follow-up. After purchase, consider sending a welcome email. Most think of a thank-you email, but a "thank you" typically signifies the end of a transaction, not the beginning of a relationship. Here are some examples:

- ⊙ *Welcome to the XYZ family/community, and thank you for trusting us with your XYZ needs.* Provide immediate contact and support information.
- ⊙ In the next message, include an educational piece or something that enhances the customer experience.
- ⊙ Continue educational content and proactive support outreach.
- ⊙ Sometime before the 30-day mark, provide another piece of educational content, and ask for feedback from the consumer.
- ⊙ At the bare minimum, touch base each quarter.

Also realize it is essential to personalize this communication. While you may send out the same message to all new customers, at least put the client's name in the email. It's so simple, but studies show that personalized emails are more likely to drive action.

Paying Attention to Your Customers's Needs

As a business, you're there to serve and support your customers, but smart businesses are also observing consumer behavior. From the Panopticon watchtower, you can see what your customers are doing with your product, how they're using it, and what they're doing with the knowledge you helped them obtain. Paying attention to what your clients are doing on social media, in their businesses, and in their successes—especially as it pertains to using your product—is vital to better understanding how to serve future customers and provide even more value to your existing consumer base.

This observation also involves understanding how current trends in industry; local, national, and global politics; and current events can impact your customer's relationship with you, your product/service, and the results they can achieve by working with you. The next step is communicating these observations and providing awareness for potential opportunities. For example, if you sell a payroll solution and you find out about a new bill that could impact how payroll is processed, tell your customers and control the narrative. State the facts, tell them you're monitoring the situation, and provide the information needed to make your customers feel that they're in the right hands.

When you can provide a value to your customer above and beyond your product, you've taken the next step in the client relationship and provided true Panopticon-style service. That's being proactive and making your communication truly dynamic.

☉ ☉ ☉

In the next chapter, we'll look at one way to have multiple touch points with your consumers—video marketing and education campaigns. As you read the chapter, think of how you can create content that will exemplify this Panopticon-style of service.

Marketing That Educates

Creating Value-Filled, Magnetic Marketing

Video Marketing

Making Kick-Ass Videos That Educate and Attract

Communicating via video is, in my opinion, one of the smartest things you can do to demonstrate your expertise. Video campaigns that aren't really marketing, but that are simply and exquisitely adding value to and educating viewers, are a key way to draw attention to your skills and expertise, leverage your credibility, and provide thought leadership.

When you educate others, you empower others. When someone is empowered by you, they remember you, the experience you provided, and how your content made them feel. That's powerful stuff. They may not be your customer at the time, but they can be an advocate for future customers. They can also be advocates for your information, sharing it with others and further establishing your credibility and expertise.

Let's take a look at dynamic communication strategies for video education campaigns and how they can help grow your business and leverage your leadership.

Video Domination

Each day there are nearly five billion views on YouTube—that's about two million views per *minute*. Add in other video sites, and those statistics go even higher. There are 300 hours of content added to YouTube every minute. In fact, by the time you're done reading this page, another 300 hours will have loaded. Holy cow! Not to mention that YouTube is the second most used search engine and the third most visited site in the world.

Are those enough statistics to justify this as a lucrative space? Good.

But with so much content being generated, the question becomes how you rise above the noise and get viewed. The answer lies in producing quality content that meets viewers' needs.

People and businesses use YouTube in various ways. Some want their videos to go viral, some want to earn advertising revenue and be seen, and others want to educate. The first two categories are rarely a success. But the third, where I feel businesses and leaders have the most potential, is still largely untapped.

Only 9 percent of small businesses are on YouTube. What I find the most interesting, though, is that between 2014 and 2015 (newer stats aren't out yet), searches for "how to" videos on YouTube increased 70 percent. *SEVENTY PERCENT!* There is a HUGE opportunity here for small businesses, large businesses, experts, thought leaders, etc., to make names for themselves by providing great value to the community.

So how can you get in on the action?

By creating a kick-ass video education campaign and communicating your value, expertise, and knowledge.

> **SPOILER ALERT**
>
> For tips on being good on camera, check out Chapter 9 on livestreaming, which also contains some useful video delivery tips.

Creating Video Campaigns That Educate and Empower

When you're creating an educational video series, you want to make sure that each video contains one clear learning point or actionable piece of advice. You want to get right to the point of the information your viewer is looking for, provide the value, answer one question (or sometimes just part of one question), and keep the video on one focus.

I call this digestible chunking (*Youtility* author Jay Baer puts it a bit more elegantly, saying that you should give away information snacks to sell knowledge meals, as you might remember from Chapter 1). Think of putting too much food in your mouth at once—you have a hard time chewing and an even harder time swallowing. It's the same with information overload in a video—it's likely to leave you focusing on the feeling of being overwhelmed, not on the content.

You want to create videos that educate and empower by making your content accessible—meaning that it's communicated in a clear, simple way that provides a path or action and that leaves the viewer feeling satisfied. Again, when you help someone help themselves, they don't forget you. Plan your content around providing value to your consumers, potential consumers, and the YouTube world in general. You may find that your audience expands as a result of people you never anticipated watching your videos. In fact, that happened to me. Let me tell you my video education marketing story.

In 2012, I decided I was going to create a campaign to end all campaigns. It was going to be solid content. It was going to educate. It was going to showcase my expertise. It was going to be spread all over. And people were going to learn my name and come knocking on my business door.

At least that's what I hoped.

I called it 60 Second Guru, *and in one minute, once per week, you could watch a new video and improve your communication and presentation skills.*

"Brilliant!" I thought. So brilliant, in fact, that I built an entire ecommerce infrastructure to sell the full series, because I just knew it would be so good that people wouldn't want to wait another week to get the rest of the series.

In September 2012 I released the first video. A year later I had sold two—yes, TWO—digital downloads and I was at a mere 60,000 views. I was pissed. I wasn't famous. I wasn't rich. This sucked.

(Okay, so I didn't quite have those delusions of grandeur, but I wasn't satisfied with the results.)

What did I do? I learned everything I could about YouTube. I dove into the analytics. I took classes. I made changes. I started researching search traffic patterns. And I adjusted my strategy. Ninety days later I went from 60,000 to 90,000 views. I did a little dance at 100,000 views. And now, approaching the 1,000,000 mark, my educational campaign has yielded some pretty nice results (in a roundabout way, the reason I'm writing this book now is because someone syndicated my videos and a publisher took notice).

I also dug deep into my analytics to discover insights on my viewership. From that I realized that a significant number (more than 60 percent) of my views were coming from outside the United States, and the search terms were largely around ESL—English as a Second Language. What did I do? I created an online product addressing business presentation skills for this audience, targeted Facebook ads to users in a specific age range in 12 countries—all backed by my YouTube data—and drove traffic to the product. An audience I never expected to have when I created my series ended up providing an additional revenue stream.

All because my content was focused on educating and adding value, and not selling myself or my services.

When you create an educational video series, the videos are *not* an advertisement for you. They *are* showcasing you as an expert. Your expertise is advertisement enough. You can have an intro/outro, show your website, etc., but a campaign around consumer efficacy is not about selling. It's about providing value that makes people want to contact you. Some of the best emails I get are the messages thanking me for my content. That person may not buy something from me that day, but they proactively reached out because something I did made a difference in their life. At the end of the day, most entrepreneurs—heck, most people I know—love getting this feedback. It's not all about the bottom line. It's about the lives you can positively impact in the process.

Strategies for Video Campaigns

There are many different strategies you can use to create a video campaign. Remember, these are audience-focused campaigns where you are providing value, not selling. Don't think that you need to come up with something new. In fact, as you'll read about soon, the existing content that you have is a great place to start when thinking about video fodder. You can also combine the strategies that are presented below to help you better educate your customers. For example, combining stories and characters with your FAQs is a great way to strategize content. Let's dive into five strategies that can help you shape your video campaigns. Remember, the goal of each video is to have a single takeaway and provide a building block for more content and value to your audience.

Top FAQs

First, think in terms of problems and solutions, questions and answers. With the massive potential to create content in the "how to" space, it's logical to think about the questions you are most commonly asked.

Get together 10 to 20 of your most frequently asked questions and start to think about creating content that answers those questions.

Look at Your Existing Content

First, look at the existing content you have: blog posts, book chapters, articles, podcasts. You likely have a lot of content produced already. How can you turn it into a video series?

If you have blog posts, you can create a video that expands on a post, adding a story or some extra example or flavor. This can help drive traffic back to your original blog posts and get people to engage (or re-engage) with your site.

FIGURE 7–1

Repurposing Sequence: Turn One Interview Into 20-Plus Pieces of Content

If you've done your own podcast, think of creating videos with the existing podcast audio. You could divide most podcasts into four or five separate videos, based on the questions asked. Add animation, images, etc., to produce creative videos that repurpose your podcast. Another way to do this is to video record the podcast, divide it up into digestible chunks of video, and then post the audio in your regular podcast locations (Figure 7-1).

If you have articles, books, contributed chapters, etc., those are all ripe for video content! Look at them and see how they can be divided, repurposed, and reinvented.

Help Your Viewer Reach a Goal

Goal-oriented videos help a viewer follow or complete the tasks necessary to reach a goal. Sometimes each video in itself can help someone reach a goal. Other times you string together a series of videos to help your audience accomplish something. This encourages more time on your site or channel and more engagement with your content. And once you help someone reach a goal, the influence principle of reciprocity kicks in, and as they've developed a relationship with you and your processes and your information, they're going to be more likely to reciprocate in some way (be that leaving great reviews, sharing your videos with others, engaging on multiple social media channels, making a purchase, sending feedback, etc.). Of course we'd like every viewer to buy something from us, but that's not the reality.

REAL PEOPLE, REAL STORIES, REAL RESULTS

Alex Charfen

CEO and Co-Founder, Charfen

Videos Need Emotional Movement and Connection

Selfie videos are the hardest videos to do. The vulnerability of one camera, no producer, no edits, just me and no improvising—it's hard. But I know a video will do well when I'm making it if I feel totally connected to the people who will be listening to it, if I'm emotionally moved as I speak. I have to put myself in the place of my audience, with those who will be watching. When I do, those videos get shared on a large scale. And live video changes everything.

The Ball Has Moved—Marketing Has Changed

If there's anybody out there who's still doing pain- or fear-based marketing, it just doesn't work in this world anymore. I want someone to have all the information they can have, and I want them to make an informed decision to work with us. Because when someone feels manipulated in a trust-based situation, you always end up kind of working from behind. It's aspirational messages that work. My videos are about how you do more, be more, see more, or identify more, and then what are the tactics around that? If the video has a positive effect on somebody, they share it. If the article has a positive effect on somebody, they share it.

It's No Longer About Pushing

I think the challenge these days is that there's been so much pushing. As a consumer, if you want to be pushed, all you have to do is walk out your front door. Today, it's highly unlikely you're going to buy something from somebody you don't trust. It's highly unlikely that you're just going to go out and land on a page somewhere and say, "Okay, this is the one." If everything you're doing is about a close, if everything you're doing is about the next purchase, you're not building a real relationship. For 99 percent of consumers, they want to know they have a real relationship first, and then they'll move forward.

If Only We All Understood How Little Everyone Else Pays Attention to Us

If entrepreneurs looked at their business and only spoke about how it mattered to others, things would change for them. Sometimes it's hard. We forget there's an audience there, and we get really caught up in our solutions and communicate detail after detail. What we want to communicate doesn't matter. What matters is what your audience needs to hear. I hear things all the time like, "I've already told him that. Why do I have to tell him again?" "You don't understand. We had a meeting last year and we went all the way through that." I always think, "If only we all understood how little everyone else paid attention to us."

Create Stories and Characters

When I think about some of my favorite YouTube videos, they all tell a story. Whether it's Henri, le Chat Noir (I love me some Henri) or learning about a new tech tool through an animated video done by Common Craft that follows a character through a short scenario, stories rule the video world.

Think about how your content can be shared through stories. You can think of case studies you've acquired, testimonials you've received, projects you've worked on. Then extract the lessons from those, create a character who is your ideal client, and tell a story that educates. You can have one character that goes throughout your videos (think of Progressive Insurance and Flo) or you can change it up every time.

Either way, you're adding character (no pun intended) to your content. That's more engaging, and we know that stories not only enhance learning, but they also increase connective power and strengthen relationships.

Themes and Categories

Organizing videos around themes and categories helps users self-select what they want to view and learn. Think of the different themes and categories that make up your expertise, and create content around those themes. Track what is being consumed and how so you can target and create new content around the themes or categories that are performing best. It's the same thing as tagging your blog posts. No matter what type of videos you create, remember to always create with the viewer in mind.

⊙ ⊙ ⊙

In the next chapter, we'll look at another way to communicate and educate—webinars. We'll talk about these from multiple angles, including lead generation, sales, support, and providing an extra revenue stream for your business.

8

Winning Webinars
Content That Sells, Converts, Educates, and Supports

A webinar is an online seminar, a synchronous event that involves both training and discussion, or some sort of interaction and engagement. It's a way for you to captivate and engage an audience. It's also a venue for interaction where you can gain valuable insights from your audience or help them come to valuable insights of their own. Since more and more businesses are realizing that their product alone is not enough to retain customers, webinars are also being provided as a way to add value to their consumer base and, in many cases, to attract new clients. Webinars are a great way to engage your employees, serve your customers, capture leads, increase sales, and (my favorite) provide an additional revenue stream.

Let's look at each benefit and talk about some communication strategies for being more dynamic when delivering webinars.

Engage Your Employees

Especially if you have a large organization or distributed and virtual teams, webinars are a great way to unite your employees and get everyone on the same page. If you have a large business and want to make everyone feel part of the experience, have a town-hall meeting via webinar or go through the same presentation you made to a board of directors or shareholders. Internal webinars are a great way to be open and build a community of trust with your employees. Since they can also be recorded, these serve as an excellent way to document organizational history to help with onboarding new employees, especially if you tag or categorize each meeting so that it's searchable. Think of a new employee being brought in to take over the lead on a project. He would be able to see what was already discussed by reviewing past internal webinars. Or a new employee wanting to see the progression of the organization over the course of a year. Now she'll have access in a way that's more than anecdotal.

Serve Your Customers

Having client-only webinars gives you an opportunity to cultivate a community around your users, who can turn into your biggest fans, advocates, and ambassadors. These webinars can be teaching them advanced tips and tricks, letting them know about new and upcoming features, giving insights, or showcasing some of the cool things your customers are doing with your product. A great strategy is to invite your customers to be guest presenters and provide case studies for implementations of your product or service. This makes them shine, it makes your product shine, and it gives your other customers ideas for how to more effectively use your product. Talk about a win-win-win!

Lead-Generation and Sales Webinars

This is one of the most common types of webinar that is offered today. This is where you get someone to register for your webinar (or a replay of your webinar) in exchange for them providing you with their email address and other relevant information. You get a new contact on your list and a chance to sell a product or service, and the prospective consumer gets free content. It's a quid pro quo exchange.

If you're using this type of webinar and want to develop a good reputation, make sure you provide content and value that can stand independent of your product or service. Focus on providing value and building a relationship so that you become the first point of contact for anyone seeking a solution in your arena.

For example, I have a client who sells life insurance. When I asked her if she had thought about using a webinar as a way to generate leads, she all but laughed at me. Her response was, "You can't use a webinar to sell life insurance." I said, "No, but you can use a webinar to educate a specific population about different life insurance policies and how they affect succession plans, and become the go-to resource on this topic."

Sure enough, she targeted solopreneurs and entrepreneurs with one to ten employees, ran an educational lead-generation webinar, and got a higher rate of conversion from lead to client than from other networking avenues. You can do this with your expertise, too!

As we've already discussed in previous chapters, there's a big gap between information and knowledge. Find a way to educate your potential consumer, position yourself as the expert resource, fill that gap, and watch your business grow.

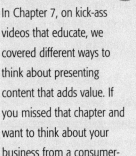

FLASHBACK

In Chapter 7, on kick-ass videos that educate, we covered different ways to think about presenting content that adds value. If you missed that chapter and want to think about your business from a consumer-education perspective, go check it out.

The One-Off For-Profit Webinar

Let's talk immediate revenue. A one-off webinar is a webinar you charge for. It's on a single topic, with a specific learning objective, a unique benefit, and a promise of value. This is not a webinar where you want to market or sell additional services. Focus instead on providing so much bang for the buck that the customer comes to you for more.

REAL PEOPLE, REAL STORIES, REAL RESULTS

David Newman

CEO and Founder, Do It! Marketing

You've Got to Get Your Mindset Right

You can pick up the feel of the entrepreneur who's running a webinar. Are they here to sell, or are they here to serve? You've got to get that serving mindset. The first impulse needs to be, "I want to help people whether they buy from me or not. I want this to be a value-rich experience." You go in with that mindset, and everything else we're about to talk about here is going to make a whole lot more sense to you.

When You Over-Teach, You Overreach

You need to figure out a very finite, very specific amount of material that you want to teach in a webinar. One of the mistakes people make is trying to teach way too much. A good webinar is depth, not breadth. If you overwhelm people and skim the surface on a lot of small issues, but never go in-depth, they'll think, "Well, you know what? I could have read a white paper. I could have found this on Google. Why did I waste my time?"

Expertise Over Information

What people are really hungry for is you as the entrepreneur, you as the expert. They don't want information. They want insight. They want opinion. They want recommendations. They want guidance. We've got to think about, what is our professional opinion? What is our slant? What is our perspective? What is our recommendation? That's way more valuable than simply information.

There's No Such Thing as a Generic Solution to a Specific Problem

People have specific problems. Your prospects, your buyers, have specific problems. There's no such thing as a generic solution to a specific problem. Our webinars have to solve urgent, pervasive, expensive, specific problems for our buyers that they will get immediate value from, again, whether they buy or not. This builds your credibility and your expertise. And this builds the relationship and trust between you and your audience.

Make Your Offer Like You're Talking to a Friend Over Coffee

At about the last 10 or 15 minutes of a 45-minute program, you comfortably, naturally, and organically pivot into an offer. You don't need to become this bizarre salesperson. A pivot statement might sound like this: "If you're serious about solving the kinds of problems we just talked about, I've got a couple of things you might want to consider as far as not only thinking about this problem, but helping you solve this problem once and for all." It's about transparency, it's about integrity, and it's about being a high-trust entrepreneur and a high-trust salesperson in every contact you make with your audience.

How do you price a one-off webinar? It depends on your audience and your topic. Even with a market saturated with "free" content, people pay for value. Focus on providing it. Think about depth in one area instead of breadth over many.

If you're going to do a one-off webinar, I suggest supplying accompanying materials, such as handouts or worksheets, that participants can use to follow along, take notes, or supplement their learning. It's also wise to leave some room for Q&A at the end. People paid for access to you, so spend a little extra time catering to your audience.

The Webinar Series

This is the crème de la crème of profit-yielding webinars; it is also the most versatile if structured and designed well.

If you're a trainer, you can use these webinars to convert your face-to-face content into a virtual format that you can sell at the same price point. If you're an author, you can expand your book into a training program that goes beyond the page. If your company offers a product that is used to help consumers generate income, specialized training webinars can be a great solution—whether or not you choose to sell them for profit. Think about a certification or continuing education units. Can your business provide content to help someone achieve a credential?

The possibilities here are endless, and the repackaging opportunities abundant. Keep in mind the importance of well-defined learning objectives, continuity of material, and making sure each module or part of the series provides value that can stand on its own, but also builds to something greater throughout the course.

Communication Strategies for Webinar Management

You've decided that a webinar is your next step. Here are some communication strategies for executing a stellar webinar.

Have Someone Checking for Engagement

When running webinars, especially if your audience is approaching (or has well surpassed) the 100-attendee mark, you want to make sure you have someone mining for questions while you're doing your presentation to send them to you for a response. Or have an assistant read the question live so you can respond right away. It's difficult to manage both presenting the information and mining for questions at the same time. Have someone help you. And be prepared to follow up on those questions that you didn't get to respond to during the webinar itself.

Don't Get Distracted by the Chat

If you allow the chatroom to be open during the webinar and people are engaging, don't allow yourself to get distracted and derail your presentation. Just as with the tip above, have someone mining the chat for relevant information and sending that to you through a back-channel chat only you can see. That way you know if something pops up there it's important.

Make Slides that Are Visually Appealing

Just like with any presentation, you don't want your PPT slides to contain too much information. If they do, people will be reading the slides instead of paying attention to what you're saying. Think of covering one main idea per slide—no more. And be sure to use images to supplement (or replace) text where appropriate. Variety in what's on the screen can help retain audience attention.

> **SPOILER ALERT**
>
> We'll talk about on-camera tips in Chapter 9, and we'll dive deep into other delivery techniques for presentations in Chapter 14. Both can definitely help with presenting webinars.

Smile, Even If You're Not on Camera

People can hear your smile through your voice. Conveying energy via a webinar is important, as you're competing with even more distractions than you would be if you were face-to-face. Present with paralanguage and emotion!

Your energy will come through, and sometimes it needs to be amped up even more when communicating through a technological channel. I know people who stand while presenting webinars. If you need to do that to get your energy right, do it. If you're using video, make sure your facial expressions are easily visible and your lighting and sound are high quality.

Vary the Status Quo Every Three to Five Minutes

If the status quo is you speaking on one slide with text only, make sure the next slide has images. Even better, toss out a polling question. Better yet, use a quick-chat strategy to engage audience members in the chat area with simple, one-letter answers (I tell them to type Y for yes and N for no). Suggest activities for them to complete or make notes to complete later. Just do *something* other than narrating a slide deck.

Use Sticky Notes for Reminders to Engage

Before each webinar, print out your slide deck. I print mine in handout form, three slides per page, and take notes on the side. If I know that I have a poll question or a quick chat question I want to ask, I put a sticky note over the slide printout to trigger the engagement activity. This way I have to physically pull the note off to get to the content on the slide. It's a pro hack for making sure you make your webinar interactive and keep your audience on course.

☉ ☉ ☉

In the next chapter, we'll dive into livestreaming and delivery skills for on-camera work. Some of these can apply to this chapter, especially if you're using video in your webinars.

Go Live!

Livestreaming Strategies and On-Camera Skills

At the time of writing this book, livestreaming is the "it" thing. By the time this is published in March 2017, there's probably going to be another "it" thing on the rise. But I'm certain that livestreaming, in some form or another, is here to stay. The access audiences desire, the transparency and vulnerability of live video, and the capability of livestreaming to provide behind-the-scenes and insider access on a large scale are all reasons this medium will last long beyond the hype.

That's why I'm writing this chapter.

If you're new to the concept of livestreaming, it's the process of broadcasting in real time via the internet. Basically, we are our own media outlets with the devices in our pockets—our phones. But just because you *can* be the media doesn't mean you should be.

If you want your business to be positively impacted by livestreaming, there's a lot more to it than taking out your phone and hitting the "broadcast" button. Let's go through some tips for planning, executing, and repurposing a livestream and talk about some on-camera delivery strategies to make your livestream communication truly dynamic.

Planning: Before the Stream

First and foremost, know that the primary purpose of livestreaming is not for selling! It's for connecting with an audience in real time. If your focus isn't on adding value to your audience, you'll lose them. Use livestream video to showcase your brand or products in a way that connects to consumers. Don't focus just on selling; focus on forming and deepening relationships with your audience, adding value to their lives, and improving their condition.

Now that we've covered that, let's talk about planning strategy.

Make Sure Your Stream Has Continuity

What does that mean? It means your livestream shouldn't exist in a vacuum apart from your business. Make sure it continues or supports your brand story. Make sure it accurately reflects a customer's experience. Make sure you're truthfully representing your organizational culture. If your business is about health and wellness, the last thing you want is a stream where you're holding a cigarette in your hand. Or even just streaming from a smoking area, with plumes filling the air. Food for thought: Don't get caught holding a proverbial cigarette!

Make Sure Your Stream Has Relevant Content

Content is queen (or king). Keep it at the top of your mind and have a clear purpose for your stream. Organize your stream, and the people and materials involved, in a way that will make sense to your viewer. Make sure your content connects to the viewer in a meaningful way. For example, simply presenting

> **SPOILER ALERT**
>
> Different ways to organize content are presented in Chapter 15, where we talk about organizing presentations—you can use the same concepts!

information on a new service, for example, isn't wise—unless you clearly state that is the purpose of your stream. However, sharing stories and interactions on how a service has helped others, while providing actionable examples, adds value to your audience and relates to who your consumers really are.

Make Sure Your Stream Is Well-Composed

This means you pay attention (and give as much forethought as possible) to the physical setting of the stream itself. What's the backdrop? What's the location? What are the parameters for the speakers? Will you stay in one place or will you be mobile? Even though a background might be cool, if it doesn't provide good lighting and, especially, acoustics, you'll need to reconsider. Be very cognizant of what is being shown in the background. I once did a video presentation from my New York City apartment, and in the middle of the call you could see someone in the building across from me walking around with his shirt off. That was a bit of a distraction to my audience! (But it makes for a good story.) Similarly, if you're streaming from your office, make sure you're not showing any proprietary information in the background of the shot. I've seen too many whiteboards pictured in office calls, and those boards sometimes contain insider information.

Make Sure Your Stream Is Well-Communicated

Make a promotion plan for your stream, and build some excitement around the event. When you write the description for the stream, set expectations. If you're going to take questions live, note that. If you're not going to be interacting with your audience, note that, too. A great pre-stream engagement and promotion strategy can involve letting your audience know that you won't be able to take live questions, but they can comment beforehand to have their question asked on the stream. Setting these expectations in your description is essential if you want to keep your audience apprised of your process.

REAL PEOPLE, REAL STORIES, REAL RESULTS

Ivonne Kinser

Director of Digital Strategy & Innovation, Avocados From Mexico

Take What You Do Locally and Amplify

If you're going to invest effort and financial resources and participate in a physical event, don't settle for staying in the local parameters. Take what you're doing and amplify it with a digital strategy on a bigger level. With everything you do that's based at a physical location, like our involvement at SXSW, take that and amplify it into the digital space—connect with audiences beyond the physical limits. Doing this, we were able to lead the digital conversation at SXSW. Us—avocados!

You Can't Increase Your Budget, But You Can Outsmart Your Competition

Partner with others to reach an audience you wouldn't otherwise reach. We may not have the big-brand budgets, but we are able to compete with, and many times beat, these big brands because we collaborate to expand our brand power. Think of who you can collaborate, partner, and align with to expand your presence. Our strengths are much bigger and better when we engage our partners in whatever we're doing, when it fits and when it's relevant, and when we share the same audiences. Partner strategically with people who can reach platforms that you, organically, can't.

Don't Let Your Landing Pages Be a Disconnect from Your Brand

A lot of traffic is driven to landing pages that are customized for specific audiences. But then they go to continue searching on the bigger website, and there is a disconnect. That's problematic. They have to see the message that speaks to them, but if they decide to keep wandering around your site, they have to feel that it's the same conversation, maybe not as relevant toward them, but it's not disconnected either.

Marketing Is Not One-Way Communication: Personalize or Die

Marketing is not like it was ten years ago. You have to listen a lot first to know how to speak to each individual. Not listening results in a generic approach. If you adopt a one-size-fits-all strategy and just deliver one message to everyone, it's not going to go anywhere. In doing this, you are saying what you want to say to everybody, regardless of who they are, what they want, or how they want to connect with your brand. This is a mistake. Allow people to connect with your brand according to their own paradigm.

Create Messages and Campaigns That Emotionally Connect
We live in a very complex ecosystem, especially in digital, and the audiences today are very fragmented. The big challenge here is how you take this overarching brand message, because to get through to your brand, it has to be one message. The best campaigns find the overarching message, dissect it, customize the communication, personalize it across the hundreds of digital platforms out there, and deliver it in a way that is highly relevant for each audience.

Make Sure to Set Goals for Your Stream

How will you measure its success? Views? Engagement? Shares? Website visits? Follow-ups on your call to action? Set your goals for each stream and take the time to review and revise.

Executing: During the Stream

A well-coordinated stream will have someone on camera as a host or main personality and someone behind the scenes. This person is mining for comments and technical issues, posting live comments and responses to questions (especially from a business perspective), and fostering the spirit of community within the live viewership. While you can do a stream on your own, having someone else managing the community engagement behind the scenes will add solid value to your viewers.

In terms of your on-stream communication, make sure you follow the expectations you communicated in the description and reiterate them during the stream for those tuning in midcourse. For example, "Just a reminder that because of the limited time we have with X, we aren't going to be able to take audience comments on the stream." Or, "Because of the stream setup today, we're not able to see comments as they come in."

Delivery-Wise, Avoid Scripts as Much as Possible

If you're reading off a script from your computer or a teleprompter, people can tell. That's not conversational. That's talking *to* someone. When you're trying to engage an audience, you don't want to talk *to* them, you want to talk *with* them. There's a big difference.

Instead, use an outline. Write down the main points you want to cover, and glance at each main point before you start talking. It's OK to look at a sheet of paper and transition. For example, "Now that we talked about X, let's go into Y . . ." and then read Y from a paper if you need to. *Do not* memorize what you're going to say. That will make you look robotic, with your eyes reading the inside of your head, searching for the next words to say, instead of you being natural and engaging on camera.

Don't Pretend to Be an Expert If You're Not One

If you do, the video will hurt your marketing and credibility more than it will help. When speaking from a knowledge position, you tend to be more conversational and sharing, instead of scripted and telling. If your stream needs to cover a topic that you're not comfortable with, bring in an outside expert or feature one of your employees who can better address the topic. It'll make both of you look good!

SPOILER ALERT

We'll talk about ways to highlight the talent in your organization in Chapter 26. Bringing your employees into a livestream is one of many ways to do that.

If you need to cover a topic on live video and you don't feel you have the expertise, bring in someone who does and do an interview. You'll still be seen as the hero for getting the information out, but the pressure will be off you to deliver all the goods. Just like dogs can sense fear, so can video viewers. If they detect nervousness or uncertainty in your delivery, they're going to doubt your information and stop watching.

Be Natural

Just as when you're speaking face-to-face, a conversational style is important. And if you stare directly into the eyes of your conversational partner—especially without blinking—you're likely to create an awkward situation. It's OK to briefly look away from the lens. It's OK to be animated. It's OK to check notes. It's okay if you make a little slip up—you are human, after all. Learn from my story.

The first time I ever recorded a talking-head video was in 2008. I was teaching a senior-level class on crisis communication at Arizona State University. I needed to miss a day of class to attend a conference, but I didn't want to cancel class or hire a substitute. Instead, I created an online lesson for my students to complete—including a short video lecture.

Knowing that eye contact is one of the most important aspects of presentation delivery, when I recorded this video on my webcam I was bound and determined to look directly into the camera and make eye contact with my audience. I made visual love to that lens.

I finished the six-minute video, uploaded it, and went on my merry way. During the next class period I asked my students what they thought of the online lesson. They were thrilled—"Why don't more teachers do stuff like that?!" "Thank you for understanding how we want to be taught." "You're awesome!"

After the fanfare subsided, a student in the back raised his hand. I called on him, and he said, "Jill, I absolutely love what you did, and I learned a lot from it, but I have one comment to share."

"Go ahead," I told him.

"With all due respect, I don't think you blinked once in the entire video, and that was kind of freaky."

The class laughed. So did I. I told him there's no way that was true, so we pulled up the video in class, watched it together, and 3 minutes and 23 seconds into the video (to be exact), I blinked.

The class cheered and laughed. We all learned a lesson.

Finally, Don't Let Your Stream Exist in Vain

Make sure you have a call to action for viewers to take after the stream is complete. Even if it's as simple as "follow" or "like" the page for notifications for future streams, or previewing what is to come, give the audience an opportunity to act. If you don't ask, how can you expect them to join in? Be sure to let your audience know the next steps.

Repurposing: After the Stream

If you stream without giving a thought to "what next?" you're missing out on some great opportunities. Think of your post-stream plan. How will you save the stream? How will you repurpose it? How will you gather data? How are you going to leverage the content? How did you measure up in terms of your engagement goals?

After the stream, be sure to edit the description, if necessary, to update the names of people involved, mention any relevant links, and provide additional resources promised. It's also a good practice, if you didn't have someone help you with this during the stream, to mine the stream for comments to see if and where you need to respond. Often opportunities to serve will present themselves here. You don't want to miss out.

> **FLASHBACK**
>
> Remember in Chapter 7 when we talked about different ways to source video content? Well, the repurposing chart I gave you there can be used for repurposing livestreams as well. Take another look at it.

Finally, evaluate and review. Watch your stream. See how you can improve. Seek feedback from trusted others. Continue to focus on making better streams to provide greater value to your audience, and smile as the results come in.

☉ ☉ ☉

In the next chapter, we'll look at a strategy for creating messages that connect with people on different levels of your audience, making sure that the message, you send are interpreted in the way you want them to be.

Oh, the Humanity!

Public Communication Strategies That Help

You Connect

CHAPTER

10

Words That Bond

Common Communication Denominators

I'm going to fly my geek flag for a bit here and toss out a phrase I've adapted—common communication denominators.

Think back to math class in elementary school when you learned to add and subtract fractions. In order to do so, you had to make sure they had the same denominator (the bottom number, as in the 2 in ½). This is known as the least common denominator—the lowest possible number that both denominators can divide into.

1/2 + 1/3 = least common denominator is 6 (2 x 3), so you have
3/6 + 2/6 = 5/6

Or, if you want to think about it in non-math terms (because I've now brought up painful memories and have scarred you), think of a common denominator as a feature shared by all members of a group.

OK. So why the heck am I talking about math terms?

Because in order to be an effective, dynamic, adaptable communicator, you need to be able to identify the common communication denominators in any audience you address.

Let's look at an example where not finding this denominator caused some employee morale issues.

A company had its year-end all-hands meeting. Everyone from the sanitation crew to the top executives, the researchers and scientists to the administrative staff, was present. At one point in the presentation, after celebrating the successes of the organization, the CEO talked frankly about the financial state of the company. In this segment, he mentioned how important it was to be cognizant of each and every expense, as the last fiscal year's revenue number was below the previous year's and expenditures were significantly higher. And because of this, they were going to be monitoring the spending in each unit more rigorously so they didn't have to go through layoffs.

That didn't set well with people, obviously, as nobody is a fan of increased monitoring, or the implication of layoffs. But what was interesting was the perception of expenditures that went through each person's head.

The executive team members were thinking that they could cut back on extravagant client entertainment and downgrade from first class to business class on flights.

The midlevel managers were thinking of ways to cut staff appreciation expenses and how to speed up processes and production to decrease overtime hours.

The entry-level staff were thinking about cutting back to drinking one cup of coffee instead of two in the breakroom each day, or maybe skipping some redundant procedures to be more efficient.

In this case, there was no common communication denominator. And you can anticipate the residual effects this caused. The CEO was not telling staff to cut back on coffee consumption or cut corners around manufacturing processes. He was trying to state that it's important for everyone to be aware of expenditures—but especially at a high level. Oops.

Unintended consequences of poor communication and failure to find common ground are damaging to both personnel and the bottom line.

Imagine another scenario at a chemical manufacturing plant (thanks to my dad—a 20-year chemical engineer—for this real-life example). The CEO had a mid-year staff meeting with the management team to review the current financials against budget. "We need to increase our profit,' he communicated. The plant's operations manager took it as we need to increase operating efficiencies and reduce unnecessary spending. The operations manager then called a staff meeting to discuss the issues with his floor supervisors. Even though improving efficiencies and reducing unnecessary spending were the points discussed, the floor supervisors interpreted that as production needs to speed up and costs need to be cut. In the spirit of following their boss's requests, the floor supervisors instructed plant operating personnel to skip over some minor safety checks to get faster production, to shortcut some of the standard operating procedures, and to cut expenditures that they didn't see as essentials. The message from the top was increased profit. The interpretation at the floor level was to cut corners and all possible costs. The result was necessary supplies not being bought, product quality compromised, and workers being put in risky situations in order to speed up processes.

If you want to connect with people and your audience, get buy-in, and motivate others to act, you need to communicate with language, examples, instructions, and details that everyone in the audience understands. You can do this by finding the common communication denominator.

Here are some ways to discover common communication denominators and get everyone on the same page.

Shared Experiences

Think of things everyone has in common. We all wake up in the morning, for example. We all eat, and each of us has a favorite drink and a favorite food. We all have people who are important to us in our lives. Tap into the experiences that we all, as human beings, share, and you'll get people on the same page. Relate those experiences to their direct roles, job tasks, or common everyday processes. Learning to tye shoes, for example, is something that everyone experienced, and now it's on autopilot. Jumping out of an airplane, on the other hand, or going on a cruise, or taking a luxury vacation, is not something that everyone can relate to.

SPOILER ALERT

In Chapter 16 we will talk about persuasive speaking and what type of messaging and delivery skills you should use to be most influential. Drawing on shared experiences to connect with your audience is just one of those skills.

Even though people may have experienced something in a different way, communicating about a shared experience is a way to tie things together. In an organization, if you had a company picnic, you can reference that event. While experiences may have been different from person to person (one person ate barbecue while another had salad), everyone shared in the same space.

Analogies are another great strategy, especially when you can combine them with shared experiences. You've likely heard "it's just like riding a bike" when someone is comparing a task you may not have done for a while to anything else you're worried you may have forgotten. Analogies are comparisons made using "like" or "as" in the context. For example, cashew butter is like peanut butter, just made with a different type of nut. Or this task is as difficult as putting toothpaste back into the tube.

Use Synonyms to Make Messages Understandable

One of the best professors I had in college has an immense vocabulary. In fact, I think I learned more words in his class than in any other throughout my degree. And they just rolled off his tongue—they weren't forced or demonstrated to show off—they were just part of his communication style. Some people found it pretentious. I thought it was amazing. Because you know what else he did? For every word that was a little difficult, he would immediately follow it with a synonym. With the synonym and in context, I was able to learn more words and how to use them.

Here's an example: "When talking about two different commercials, if you watch them both and juxtapose, or contrast, the way each brand uses the color red, you'll see some stark differences." In this case juxtapose is the $3.50 word and contrast is a synonym. So if you don't know the big word, you can still understand it by the context and the synonym.

Brilliant!

You can also use this strategy when explaining jargon or acronyms, as presented in the next section.

I've since used this technique in speeches, writing, training, etc., over the years with much success. Thanks, Dr. Kelly McDonald. You made me smarter and make my clients happier.

Jargon and Acronym Suicide

Don't assume your industry's or company's jargon or acronyms are known by your audience—even if your audience members are in the same industry or even the same company! This is one of those situations where ass-u-me really comes into play. If you're a leader and you make the assumption that everyone knows something, you won't be seen as accessible. If you're an employee and you don't understand an acronym, you might feel like an ass (or maybe an idiot) if you have to raise your hand and ask.

Don't put anyone in that position!

In business, if you're having an all-hands meeting and talking about a project that the entire room isn't familiar with, make sure it's fully explained. If you're using industry jargon that not everyone in the room would know, be sure to use a synonym with it. If you're using acronyms, spell them out the first time unless you're 100 percent certain that everyone is on the same page. Don't trust that people will ask if they don't understand—they probably won't. And then you'll have a message that's lost in translation and an action that may not be taken or taken correctly.

REAL PEOPLE, REAL STORIES, REAL RESULTS

Adam Elsesser

CEO, Penumbra

You're a Human . . . Talk Like One

People in business tend to use jargon. No one responds to that. I don't respond to that, so why would I expect anyone else to respond to those types of terms? You have to talk about what you do in the most fundamental terms. Express things the way you would if you were a real human being—because you are! When you do, it just becomes part of communicating in the culture of a company.

Failure Is Part of the Process When It Comes to Innovation

One of the most important things when you are trying to build a company based on constantly making innovative products is to remember that if you're going to do something that's never been done before, you're going to fail along the way. As companies grow, they tend to become more risk averse. Know that working on things that don't always work is not a negative. You have to give your employees, and yourself, permission to fail. And that permission needs to be clearly communicated.

Don't Talk in Terms of Market Opportunity, Talk in Terms of People

When we first went public in 2015, one of the people advising us was trying to frame our story in terms of market size and market opportunity. Buzzwords. I was a little taken aback—I've never talked about what we do in terms of a market opportunity, because we're talking about individual patients and people. Let's talk about the number of people we can positively impact. That gets you to the same message, but it keeps it in the way of thinking that reflects our culture.

Get People on the Same Page with Onboarding Communication

I have a ten-year tradition of meeting every week with all new employees. No matter their role in the company, they all come together and I describe why we started the company, the goal of making products that impact clinical outcomes, and some of the patients I have met and what they've said to us as a company. I describe our culture—a focus on the outcomes of our products and the people we serve. Many people choose to work with us because of that direct connection that their work has on patients every single day.

Stop Tiptoeing and Be Painfully Direct

There's a sense that when you talk about what's happening at a company, particularly if you're the CEO or a senior executive, that you have to say things that are scripted. That's the biggest mistake: tiptoeing around issues, especially in terms of performance. Performance conversations can be seen as difficult, but almost every one of those conversations can end with the person being incredibly happy that these issues are finally being pointed out and that there is a pathway to improving and succeeding in what they do. Sometimes, they just didn't know how to get there.

Even if someone does know what an acronym means, sometimes the time they need to process that meaning will interrupt their stream of consciousness, whereas you've already moved on to your next point. By the time it "clicks" in their mind, they've already lost track of their place in the conversation.

Colloquialisms and Conversational Language

Let's talk about a fun word. Colloquialism. I'll say it again, because it's fun to say. Col-lo-qui-al-ism. When we speak colloquially, we use common everyday words: slang, clichés, and a conversational style. It's the language of the common man.

However, I know many executives who intentionally avoid using common language, instead obfuscating relevant information from getting through. (Oh, I just did that, didn't I . . . obfuscating means to intentionally block, be ambiguous, or make difficult to understand.) That's a power play. And it's not cool.

Many people think when they're giving a business presentation that they shouldn't be colloquial, and that's flat out not the case. Of course, you need to analyze your audience beforehand, but for your average audience situation you're going to want to use language that shows you understand and can relate to them, and sometimes colloquialisms help you do just that. Consider integrating a conversational style into your presentations. Think of a give and take between you and the audience. Some of the best presentations I've ever seen have used that conversational style to interact with their audience, pose questions, elicit responses, and drive action.

Using colloquial language in your presentation makes you appear less like somebody preaching from a stage and more like someone truly interacting with your audience. Obfuscating or intentionally confusing language makes people wary. In order to generate action and results with your communication, you need to gain trust. People don't trust people they can't understand. Keep it simple. Keep it conversational. Keep it colloquial.

☉ ☉ ☉

In the next chapter, we'll cover situations where the common communication denominator can really help you foster relationships that can grow your business—networking and pitching.

Surround Yourself with the Right People

Networking and Your Pitch

If you want to succeed in business, you need to surround yourself with the right people. But finding those people is not easy.

When we think about surrounding ourselves with the right people, we often think in terms of what those people can do for us. However, that's a short-term viewpoint. The real question you should be asking is: "What value can I bring to people?"

People do business with people, not businesses. Most people at networking events go right out, shake hands, ask what the other person's name and business are, and hand off a card. Sound familiar? If so, smack your business-card-passing hand on the wrist!

That, my friends, is *not* how connections are made. Aim for the "second handshake" with your networking conversations. What is a second handshake? I'm glad you asked.

Picture this scenario: You walk into a networking event, and as usual, people are looking at you like you're their next meal. Someone immediately approaches you, reaches out to shake your hand, and says (in one breath), "Hi, my name is Brady, I'm the owner of Awesome Business, I do X, Y, and Z. What's your name and what do you do?" You spurt your scripted answer back, exchange cards, and walk away. There is no connection; there is no second handshake.

Now, try this scenario: You walk into a networking event, go up to someone who looks interesting, shake hands, and introduce yourselves by name. You say, "Phil, I'm curious—how did you get into doing what you do?" And a conversation ensues. After about five minutes, you've learned that you both left corporate jobs to go it on your own. You have something in common. The foundation of a relationship is laid. And you both genuinely enjoyed the conversation to the point that when you start to walk away, he extends his hand and gives you a second handshake. Success!

If you approach networking and relationship building in this manner, you're bound to get a second handshake.

It's these conversations—these second handshakes—that are the foundation of mutually beneficial relationships. The relationships that allow you to surround yourself with the right people. The relationships that lead to business success.

Questions to Get a Conversation Started

Need some help getting that conversation going? Here are some questions you can ask that will likely throw someone a little off their pre-scripted networking pitch game. By doing that, you're likely to have a better conversation, find a connection, and get that second handshake.

Business-Oriented Questions

- ⊙ How did you get started in this industry?
- ⊙ Why do you love to do what you do?
- ⊙ How do you spend your time? (Courtesy of Dan Meredith)
- ⊙ What's your favorite type of client to work with?
- ⊙ What's your favorite problem to solve?
- ⊙ What's the first thing you do when you sign a new contract?

- ⊙ What's your favorite way to celebrate success?
- ⊙ What is something a client has said to you that really made you happy?

Digging Deeper and Some Atypical Questions

- ⊙ When you were a little kid, what did you want to be when you grew up?
- ⊙ What was your favorite toy as a child?
- ⊙ (As a follow-up) Does it connect in any way to what you do today?
- ⊙ What is your favorite holiday tradition that you celebrate with friends, family, or your employees?
- ⊙ What's something you're most looking forward to doing with your business (or with your family) in the next year?
- ⊙ What do you feel has been the secret to your success?

Use these questions to help generate conversations and see what type of relationships can develop!

REAL PEOPLE, REAL STORIES, REAL RESULTS

Dorie Clark

Entrepreneur, Author of *Reinventing You* and *Stand Out*

Networking Serves Dual Purposes

When it comes to becoming known in your industry, your network is critical, because it actually serves multiple purposes. One is social proof. You're known by the company you keep. If you're aspiring to be a leader in a certain field and no one else in that field has heard of you, that's generally a problem. The other is that networking is a way of building relationships with people who could be early ambassadors for your idea. These are the folks who can really help your ideas get better, get refined, and get spread.

The "Let's Grab Coffee" Meetings Can Be Inefficient

Anytime someone becomes reasonably advanced in their profession, you get many requests for your time. It becomes enormously overwhelming—you cannot possibly have coffee with everyone who wants to do it. It would kill all your time. Instead, host a networking dinner. Pick a date, a place, and eight to ten people. It's more efficient, and everyone will get more value. You get to know them. You get to know other people. They get to know you and other people. It's a network effect.

Friends First, Business Second

Where people go wrong is they think of networking as being so hyper-transactional, and then it feels icky to them. Of course it does if you're just looking for a target to get something from. Don't even think about that initially. You need to look for friends first. If you can find someone you're really simpatico with, regardless of how relevant their business seems to you, that's a win. They're at a business networking event. They know people. They have friends. They have colleagues. And now you'll have a new friend, too.

Don't Forget the Follow-Up

The sexy part of networking, the part that everyone focuses on too much, is the top of the pipeline—where you're meeting new people. But the part that actually is more valuable that people forget is lower down in the pipeline. Once you've met someone, what do you do? Most don't ever do anything, and then they just lose all those connections. It's like it never happened. Get better at following up with the ones you meet, and turn them into real connections and real relationships.

Find the Facts That Help Advance a Conversation

You want to give people as many hooks as possible in your introduction. That means you should present facts about yourself that give listeners something they can latch onto and find a commonality or something to talk to you about. Maybe it's a hobby. Maybe it's a cool client. People will either have something to say because they also do that and they think it's cool, or they'll just have a lot of questions about it. Either way, it makes you easy to talk to, and that's all you need at that point.

Bridging the Friend Gap

Sometimes your best networking can be within your circle of friends and family. Especially when you're first starting out, you need to tap into the existing resources at your disposal. But it's often difficult to approach a friend and ask for connections. Let's chat about communication strategies you can use to ask friends for help without taking advantage of the friendship or seeming like you're using them.

Let's say your friend works for a company that you're dying to get into and pitch. They'd be your perfect client and you know you could add considerable value to their business. However, you've never really done business around this friend before. She's never seen you in action. She doesn't know any of the clients you've gotten results for. She doesn't have a professional frame of reference for you.

If this is the case, you're likely not going to go straight up to her and say, "Hey, introduce me to your CEO."

That takes advantage of the friendship, it's a little sketchy, and unless your friend has personally seen you in action or has used or knows someone who has used your product, it's a bit of a reach to ask for a firsthand referral or introduction. Instead, have a conversation with your friend to find out more about the company and its culture. Ask questions about processes and procedures. Inquire about struggles and challenges. Try questions like: "In your industry, what are some of the challenges you see? Is there a big difference between upper management and non-management, or even midrange managers, in the company you work for? What are some of the frustrations you experience in your job?"

From that, you're learning her experience in her organization, so if at some point along the line, you feel you could help, you would have a conversation point to reference. If you're trying to get information to figure out how to better approach a company, you can check for understanding to make sure you've gotten a clear picture.

Turning some of your friend conversations into more professionally driven conversations, as long as there is a genuine interest in learning the information and not just pitching, is another way you can leverage your existing network.

The (Dreaded) Networking or Elevator Pitch

Many small business owners, especially those who serve a local area, find a lot of benefit in joining networking and referral groups. These groups can often be found in your local chamber of commerce or in organizations such as BNI—a group for business networking and referrals.

In networking situations like these, you'll be asked to deliver a 30- to 60-second pitch. In many cases you'll be timed, and going over can hurt your credibility. Therefore, it's important to have a pitch prepared for these situations, and it can benefit you if you have a pitch that's unique, stands out from the crowd, and isn't the same run-of-the-mill pitch you'll likely hear everyone else give.

A standard pitch with a networking referral group sounds like this:

Hi, my name is [insert name].

I'm with [insert company].

And we have this slogan: [insert slogan].

And we do this [states products or services].

A good referral for me this week is [insert referral request].

I'm [name].

I'm with [insert company].

And we have this slogan: [insert slogan].

Groan. Snore.

Think any of that is going to motivate someone to refer business to you? Unless you have a killer differentiator, not likely. The reality is this: You have 30 seconds to pique your audience's interest. You're not going to make a sale in 30 seconds. At best you'll strike a chord with someone in the room and she will want to talk to you later.

SPOILER ALERT

Great tips for effective delivery and persuasive impacts for your pitch and presentations are coming up in Chapters 14 and 16.

But what if that didn't have to be the case? What if you could not only strike a chord but also be remembered and have you and your business be at the top of the mind for many people in the group? What if you could find a way to connect with another person to start a bigger conversation—which is really the whole point? Let's look at a pitch done differently, a pitch that can deliver these results.

The Pitch That Gets Remembered

Relationships are built based on shared experiences and connections, not a bulleted list of facts and slogans. Pitches that get remembered tell a story. They deliver a narrative about you, your business, what you do, why you do it, the people you serve, and the results you get. It's a short story that gets to the heart of your business and the value you provide. But, more important, it gets straight to the point of the change you produce and the clients you serve.

So how do you get to these shared experiences and create connections in a 30-second pitch?

By telling a story that leaves people both complete and curious at the same time. It's a tall order, but it can be done. You need to get across the idea of what you do, but you need to leave room for questions and conversation to emerge. You want to say enough that those who are interested will approach you and those who aren't will still remember you. Figure 11.1 on page 102 is an activity you can do that will help you get to the main values and benefits your business provides, and help you think about a few stories along the way.

Once you've done this brainstorming exercise, you'll have some words to use in your pitch that will be consistent and meaningful. Next, think of the stories you can tell that lead you to those words, and how you can tell a piece of that story to intrigue the listener or help strengthen your pitch. Here's an example.

It costs more to get a new customer than it does to retain an existing client. Yet most companies are more focused on sales than retention. I'm Jill Schiefelbein, and I create strategies to help companies retain clients. Take my SaaS client, who came to me with a 5% conversion rate after a free trial period. By implementing an educational video and communication campaign, we jumped from 5% to 20% conversion to paying clients. If you know a company that needs help educating and retaining customers, I create strategies to make that happen.

Compare this to the earlier script and you'll see the differences.

Values and Benefits Activity

Materials
- Four sheets of paper
- Writing utensil
- Timer
- 25 to 30 minutes of your time to focus

Take one sheet of paper and write at the top:

Who am I?

Set a timer for five minutes. Write as many responses to the question as you can in those five minutes. Think of who you are as an individual, as a business owner, as an employee. Remember, people do business with people! These are the things that make you who you are. They don't need to be complete sentences—they can be words and phrases. Write for the entire five minutes. When the timer's up, stop.

Set that sheet aside. Grab a second sheet. At the top of this page, write,

Who do my customers say I am?

Set the timer for five minutes again. Start writing as much as you can to answer this question. What do your customers say about you? What feedback have you heard? What value did you provide? Again, write for the entire five minutes. Even if you find yourself being repetitive, that's OK. Keep writing!

FIGURE 11–1
Values and Benefits Activity

Values and Benefits Activity

When the time is up, set the sheet aside and grab the third one. On this page, write,

What is in it for the potential consumer?

Another way to think of this question from the consumer's frame of mind is "WTF should I care?" What's in it for them? How are you different from anyone else? What would make you the best choice? Set the timer for five minutes and write, write, write. This one is likely going to be a bit harder. But here's a hint—when you connect who you are with what you do and then focus on the results you're capable of providing, it gets a little easier.

Finally, set the sheet aside and get the last blank piece. On this page, write,

What do you want me to do and why?

This is also from the consumer's perspective—what do you want them to do? Set the timer. Go! Write as much as you can in five minutes about what action you want the consumer to take. This is your call to action. You need a tangible call to action that people can actually, well, act on—tell us to actually go with you, act with you, talk to you, whatever it may be. If you don't have a call to action in your pitch, you're just delivering information.

When the timer is up, set the four sheets side by side. Look at the sheets and circle or highlight any words or phrases you see repeated. These words and phrases are likely tied to your core values or the unique differentiators that you can bring to add value to your customer. This gives you a starting point for words to use when making a pitch.

FIGURE 11–1

Values and Benefits Activity, continued

11 / Surround Yourself with the Right People

⊙ ⊙ ⊙

In the next chapter, we discuss strategies for communicating with the media and for being a great interviewee. We'll also touch on another type of pitch—pitching the media. Some of the words you discovered by reading this chapter may help you in your media responses, so don't forget them!

Hot Off the Presses

Media, Stories, and Spreading the Word

It's said that no press is bad press. But any press can be a missed opportunity if you don't come to the table armed and ready to play. Especially for new and budding companies, press coverage in the right outlets is hugely important. It helps you build your brand and your credibility with all audiences and provides that all-important social proof that helps drive people to your proverbial front door.

If you want to make the media your friend and build a connection with reporters that will keep you and your business in a positive light, here are some things you need to do. I'm presenting them in a rapid-fire format so you can get right to the point and get right to good press.

The strategies in this chapter are for how to communicate once you get the interview. For strategies on getting the interviews in the first place, I interviewed not just one, but two media experts for this chapter.

REAL PEOPLE, REAL STORIES, REAL RESULTS

Jess Todtfeld

CEO and Founder, Success in Media

Kate Delaney

Speaker and NBC Radio Personality

Get Booked by Being Buzz Worthy

Kate: You become buzz worthy when you can plug in to whatever it is people are talking about in a 24-hour period. That's an easy way to get booked with your expertise. You need a "wow," something that attracts the media to why they would want to book you. Make your expertise match with current events in a way that is relevant to the media you're pitching.

You Have to Walk in the Shoes of the Person You're Pitching

Kate: Every day, I get more than a hundred pitches from people who are talking about their book, their idea, their event coming up, from people thinking they're doing something so awesome that they can't imagine how anyone in the media wouldn't want to cover it. Usually they know zero about me. They have no idea what I cover on the show and they've already pitched me something that in no way would fit. It's a bad pitch.

Winging It Is Not a Strategy

Jess: What happens is when they go out and they try to get a media interview, initially they say, "I'm doing it because I want to promote my business. I want to take myself to the next level." The day the interview comes along, the bar drops all the way down to "I just don't want to look stupid." That is OK, but that's not the goal we should have. We could do so much better than that, and people just say, "Well, there's so much on my mind. I just figured I'd wing it." Don't wing it. Be smart, prepare yourself, use the strategies in this chapter. Make yourself great.

Once You've Answered a Question, You Have Control

Jess: If you're still talking, you can bring the conversation over to what you want to talk about by building on what they asked. Give a short answer that deals with the question directly, and then give the long answer, which is bringing it on over to things you talk about and what is relevant to the audience. A media appearance should satisfy three parties—the media, the audience, and you!

Here Is Every Question You Will Ever Get Asked

Jess: Every question you will ever get asked in an interview, ever, will involve one of these: Who, What, Where, When, Why, or How. Prepare yourself by practicing answers to the WWWWWH questions about your topic and about any current events you're relating your topic to. The best way to practice is with a recording device—video or audio, depending on the media—so you can review and improve.

Interview Etiquette

You've got the interview. Now what? For starters, here are some basics that will help you get in the right frame of mind to ensure that not only you deliver a great interview, but that you'll be high on the media's list for being asked back.

Say Please and Thank You

It's simple, right? But how many people forget to do it, or don't do it proactively? A ton. And it's sad. Can you imagine changing the script on a reporter?

What would it be like if, before a reporter asks you a single question, you say: "Thank you for letting me share with your audience." I guarantee you that many have never heard a proactive, pre-interview thank-you before.

The after-interview words of thanks are much more common, but you shouldn't forget! Yes, you are helping the reporter by giving him sound bites for a story, but he is also helping you by putting your face and words out there. So thank him for that! You'll be surprised at the difference it can make once you do it consistently.

Be Helpful

As the interview reaches its end, ask: "Is there anything else I can talk about or answer that will help with your story?"

Doing this during a live interview while the camera is rolling probably isn't the best strategy. But as you're shaking hands to part ways, ask.

If a reporter knows you are willing to work *with* her, you're more likely to get requested for interviews in the future. And, who knows, you might get an additional feature right on the spot! This also shows you respect what the reporter is doing as a profession. And that never hurts!

Follow Through

This is simple. If you say you're going to do something, do it. We all know someone who is all talk and no action. Don't be that person.

It's just like that colleague who brags constantly but never delivers results or has anything to back it up. Nobody likes or will rely on that person.

The same goes with the media. If you say you'll give an interview and then don't, or try to rush through it, your actions speak louder than your words and you are going to be viewed as someone who doesn't keep her promises. And you don't want to move the media out of your corner. Your business can't afford it.

Reciprocity: Share the Love

If a reporter does a special story about you, puts it out via social media, and "tags" or "tweets" you in any way, share it with your followers and fans. This simple act will endear you to reporters near and far, as they realize you're conscious of what is put out about you in the media and you're happy to share their work.

Think of it this way: When you and your business put out articles, information, celebrations, and other material into the social realm, don't you feel good when you see people replying, retweeting, favoriting, or sharing it in some way? I bet so! Reporters are people, too. This will go a long way toward developing relationships.

On the Record

Words have immense power. And when you're being highlighted by the media, your message has the potential to reach far and wide. Here are some tips to help your interview be more relatable to the audience and make your business shine.

> **SPOILER ALERT**
>
> In Chapter 14, we'll cover more strategies for effective delivery that you can use in media and interview situations, as well as in the boardroom, with your employees, on a big stage, and the list goes on.

Speak Clearly

Ever say something you wish you could take back? Most of us have. When you're in the limelight, your words are magnified even more.

That's why any slip of the tongue can get you in trouble and hurt not only your own reputation, but the reputation of your brand or organization as well. And it's not just saying something politically incorrect or taboo that can get you in trouble. You can also get a negative image by speaking poorly.

If you've never seen a video of or listened to yourself giving an interview, you need to do so immediately. Put down this book now and do it. Was it painful? Was it OK? How did you feel? Did you see areas for improvement but don't know how to improve?

We are our own worst critics. But in this day and age, if you sound like an idiot in an interview, it's instantly all over the media, Twitter, Facebook, and YouTube—your inarticulateness in all its glory. If you have the tendency to stammer or use filler words (um, uh, so, like, hmmm, etc.), you need to learn to do one thing. Pause.

Yes, it's that simple. You do not need to be uttering sound the entire time during an interview. A pause can be purposeful, strategic, and helpful. A pause will keep you from spitting out those words that have no purpose.

Reporter: After a great first year with substantial growth, what does the next year look like for AWESOME BUSINESS XYZ?

The Boss: Well, man, it's, uh, going to be great, man, and I'm, uh, ready to get started. We have, you know, a lot of talent in our organization, man, and, uh, our customers are fantastic. It's going to be a fun challenge, uh, to see how much more we can grow and continue to provide, uh, quality products, man.

Now, let's look at this without filler words.

Reporter: After a great first year with substantial growth, what does the next year look like for AWESOME BUSINESS XYZ?

The Boss: It's going to be great. I'm ready to get started. We have a lot of talent in our organization, our customers are fantastic, and it's going to be a fun challenge to see how much more we can grow while continuing to provide quality products.

Notice the difference? So does everyone else.

Repeat the Question

A common strategy used in many interview situations to buy time and clarify meaning is repeating the question. I'm not talking word for word, but if you paraphrase the question back to the reporter, you give yourself some time to think about your response, take a breath, and answer intelligently. You also make sure that the question you are responding to is the one that is being asked.

Have a Conversation

An interview is a conversation, plain and simple, but so many people don't think of it that way. If you want to hug people with words, you have to be yourself. You have to tell stories. And you have to do it in a conversational way.

An interview is a two-way street. The reporter may ask you a question to get it started, but you have the power to change the course of the interview through your answers. Don't think of it as a simple Q&A session. Think of it as an opportunity to share some of yourself, get to know the reporter, and find a good conversational rhythm.

It's true—not all reporters are created equal, and some are easier to talk to than others. But if you approach each reporter with the attitude of, "Hey, let's have a conversation about [insert topic of interview]," instead of, "I have to answer a few questions about this," you'll see great results.

Storytelling Is Captivating

For me, one of the best parts of kindergarten was story time. I loved listening to stories about animals and dragons and superheroes and other beloved characters.

As an adult, I love listening to people tell their stories about why they do what they do and how they got to where they are in life.

When I listen to these stories, I find ways to connect and identify with the storyteller. Ever have one of these connections? That is *exactly* how you can hug people with words—by telling stories.

As I mentioned in Chapter 10, audiences are drawn to people with whom they can identify. If your story has something in common with a member of your audience and you share it, you've made a connection. If you don't share your story, you miss out on an opportunity.

You don't have to have a long, drawn-out story to share. Short, simple stories that give people a glimpse into your personality and your life are important. It's easy to slip a short story into an interview.

SPOILER ALERT

Hug people with words? What does that mean? Well, it means that people feel such a connection with what you're saying that it almost feels like a verbal hug. I'll explain this more in terms of its importance to persuasive presentations in Chapter 16.

No Man Is an Island

The line between what is public and private is becoming increasingly blurred. Often our personal and professional lives merged together, as our businesses become our lives, and our employees our friends. Here are interview tips to keep in mind when others are involved.

Know Your Surroundings

The world is a stage, and you're a constant performer. With technology so easily accessible, anyone can be standing behind you with a smart phone ready to record your every word.

Think you're having a private party with friends? Unless you can trust them all 100 percent, you can't put anyone on blast or throw out slang that would be offensive to others—especially your employees, customers, and investors.

Is this fair? It doesn't matter. It's reality. If you don't want your words to hurt you, your business, and your chances for growth, you need to pay attention to your surroundings, and know when you're in a place where you can speak freely and when you're in a place where you might need to be more guarded. It's not ideal. I'm just keeping it real.

Thank Your Employees/Customers/Supporters

These people are already on your side, so some entrepreneurs take them for granted. But if you want to get in good with your support base, always make it a point to thank them in your interviews. Plus, it makes you appear gracious, kind, and appreciative.

We wouldn't be in the position we are today without our (customers/ employees/supporters).

The reason we've grown so much in the past year is because of the extreme dedication and talent of our (customers/employees/supporters).

I'm so grateful for our (customers/employees/supporters).

Because, really, without their support your business wouldn't exist. So acknowledge that immediately. It's an excellent dynamic communication strategy to build relationships across all three audiences, and it's the truth.

In a similar light, if your business wins an award, it's always good to acknowledge your fellow nominees and their efforts. And if you don't win the award, respect the winner. Whatever you say, genuinely mean it.

Talk About "We," Not "Me"

Nobody likes an egomaniac. Before you go into an interview, check your ego at the door. The media is not a place for arrogance—unless, of course, arrogance is your brand.

You've probably heard the saying, "There's no 'I' in 'team.'" So turn your "me" statements into "we" statements, which acknowledge that you are part of a greater whole—part of a business team.

Listen to how this sounds.

Reporter: This was a tough quarter for Awesome Business XYZ.

The Boss: Yeah, I worked as hard as I could but sometimes it isn't enough. My business isn't doing as well as I would like. I need to figure a process out. I need to make some changes.

Sound a little self-absorbed? Here's how you can turn this "me" focus into a "we" response.

The Boss: We did have a tough quarter, but that doesn't mean that the whole team at Awesome Business XYZ didn't come to the table with their best. Some situations are beyond our control, but together we've set up a great process to exceed our goals next quarter.

Much better! Changing the pronouns makes a difference. Don't underestimate that.

Publicly Thank, Recognize, and Encourage

Most people like to be recognized when they do well. I'm sure you like to know when you've given a great presentation, exceeded a sales goal, or made a customer happy. Your clients and supporters are no different.

If someone does something nice for you, thank him. If someone goes out of her way to make a media appointment easy for you, recognize the effort. If someone tells you that you are a role model, encourage him to keep working hard.

But how do you do this publicly? You can use social media, and you can use your interviews!

If a client did something really nice for you or got killer results from using your product or service and shared that with you, acknowledge that story and thank that client in your interview. Then share that interview on social media, tagging the client and/or featuring that client in a blog post that links to the interview. Even a simple mention on social media sites can go a long way. The audience will love hearing an off-the-cuff story and real-world example, and that client will remember you forever. Those stories make for easy sound bites that reporters can run over and over again and that media outlets can put on websites and social media channels. Doing a little good can go a long way.

☉ ☉ ☉

In the next chapter, we'll talk about communication strategies you can use with the media, your internal audience, and your customers when things maybe aren't going as well—in other words, when an organizational crisis hits.

When the Sh*t Hits the Fan

Communicating During a Crisis

While you hope to never experience a crisis situation in your business, it's important to be prepared. Consider your crisis communication strategy a communication insurance policy you can pull out of your back pocket if something happens. Of course, managing a crisis isn't as simple as it's presented in this chapter—in fact, I could write a whole book just on crisis management and communicative responses—but there are some key elements that every business owner and manager needs to understand when forming and communicating a response during a dynamic, ongoing situation.

An organizational crisis can take many forms—from natural disasters (earthquake, flooding, tornadoes, etc.) to unforeseen events (attacks, fire, explosion, etc.) to human error (product recall, technical outage, hiring the wrong person, acting dishonestly, etc.). Natural disasters and unforeseen events are often covered in business contracts under a *force majeure* clause. Literally, force majeure means something caused by a superior force. For your contracts, it means something that could not reasonably be foreseen or prevented. When used in a contract, it basically removes liability from both parties if an event or extraordinary circumstance, such as a natural disaster or state of emergency, prevents those contracted from completing the obligations in said contract. Sometimes the contract is canceled in full, but more likely the contract is extended or put on pause. In most cases, human error does not all under *force majeure*, making a solid crisis communication strategy even more important.

No matter what type of organizational crisis you experience, it's important to be as proactive as possible with your communication and ensure that you make the necessary apologies, changes, and adjustments to whomever is impacted by the event. If your business experiences a crisis, here are three stages you can examine to help you craft a response.

Sh*t Just Got Real

Crisis communication used to be managed differently. You used to have a little time to formulate a response and get everyone on the same page. But now, with the immediacy of social media and the ability of your consumers, employees, and bystanders to upload and distribute information at the tap of a screen, you need to respond right away.

As soon as you know something is wrong, be as proactive as possible. It's much better for you and your business if you break the news, rather than someone else letting it slip via social media, which is then picked up by the larger media.

Also, be aware that everything—and I mean *everything*—that precedes and follows is available for public consumption. Every channel your brand/business is on is a channel that customers and the public can use to reach you to judge and complain and applaud your actions or inactions. Every tweet you've been mentioned in before, during, and after the crisis unfolds will be scrutinized, along with every snap that gets chatted and every gram that gets posted. And all along, of course, there's livestreaming capturing it in real time.

This is a double-edged sword. On the one hand, every mistake you make is magnified. On the other, everything you do well has the

REAL PEOPLE, REAL STORIES, REAL RESULTS

Brooks Thomas and Derek Hubbard

Social Business Team, Southwest Airlines

Train Your Teams to Respond

Everybody who touches our social account goes through a specific set of training to help them understand the voice and tone of our social channel, and then how they can really put that voice into those responses. Our customer care team listens to our social channels, and it's their responsibility to be able to listen to what the customers are saying and respond and assist them. It's all about how we can listen to what people are saying and provide them actionable help.

Both Your Customers and Your Employees Need to Identify with You

Passion is a currency, so when you talk about transactional messaging, it needs to be bolstered, especially in a live sense, with authenticity really going into those moments and drawing out the emotion. Before we ask you to buy a ticket, we're going to go live with a purpose to show you something, or to really get you emotionally invested. Corporate social responsibility is about doing things in an authentic and transparent way, where not only the customer can identify with you, but the employee will, too.

Being Human Is the First Thing We're Going to Do

When our systems went down in July 2016, we knew we had a pretty wide-scale event on our hands. Our concern was, how do we need to own this on the Southwest front? How can we look at this from the emotional lens of what a customer is feeling in the airport, what an employee is feeling, and then how this is all working together, and how do we put that into our communication? We needed to go out there and continue the narrative of showing what we've done and what we're going to do.

The More Transparent, the More the Emotional Tone Shifts

Instead of giving any one media the exclusive, we decided we'd give everyone the exclusive. We'd go live. It really was the most utilitarian thing we could do. Our CCO was the first to go live, and immediately apologized. There wasn't a lot of information that we could say, other than, "We're hard at work. We are so, so sorry, not just to our customers, but to our employees," because our employees got dealt an equally poor hand as the customers did. Every time we went live, we felt the emotion and the tone turn a little bit.

Good Stories Beget Good Stories

When you show people doing something in an authentic way, other people come out of the woodwork to reinforce that with their own stories. During our major outage, humanity and people's respect for one another came out. Stories about making the best of a bad situation emerged with employees serving pizza at gates, step lines performing in airport terminals, impromptu talent shows being organized, Cub Scouts setting up tents. When we're talking about being progressive as a company, that was as much validation as we needed.

potential to make it into the public sphere. When you're thinking of your immediate response, keep in mind that facts are incredibly important.

Response Strategy

If the crisis is a result of a natural disaster, state of emergency, or other unforeseen catastrophic event, your initial response statement should include a clear explanation of what your company is doing to manage operations, keep customers safe (both physically and digitally in terms of data), and the expected path to recovery. In these situations, likely your company had and has no control over the event itself, but that doesn't dissipate the frustrations of customers in the moment, and them publicly airing these frustrations.

Think of when you experience travel delays due to a minor storm. It's frustrating! And a lot of people post publicly about that—but they don't complain about the storm; they complain about their airline. "Darn (airline). Another delayed flight." It's not the airline's fault the storm hit, but they received negative exposure on social media because of it. Or think of when a natural disaster hits and that item you ordered from Amazon gets delayed because shipping channels had to be rerouted. Amazon will still take some heat from angry customers, even though it wasn't at fault.

Another strategy to use in this type of crisis is to identify with your audience as much as possible—show how you're all on the same team or in the same proverbial boat.

If the crisis is a result of human error within your organization, this is when you likely have the most to lose. Owning responsibility is almost always the way to go here. An immediate gut response is to create a scapegoat. I urge you to reconsider that strategy. Even if the crisis is a result of one person's actions, the system that allowed the actions to occur, and the system that hired that person in the first place, will come under scrutiny. Just as sound doesn't occur in a vacuum, neither does human error occur in isolation.

If you have identified the person or persons responsible and have decided to place blame early on, then state the facts up front and in detail. Attributing blame directly is a big leap, so be sure you're ready to take it. And then be prepared to handle the fallout on a systemic level—how the employee was hired in the first place, what conditions must have existed to allow the person to make the error, what the organization could have done to prevent the situation. While should'ves, could'ves, and would'ves aren't the healthiest scenarios to get stuck pondering, you can bet your next paycheck (or contract) that the public sphere will be all over them. Owning up to the facts and stating your plans to examine how the crisis occurred is important. If you're caught in a lie, or even in a slightly stretched truth, the world will eventually find out and you will suffer the consequences.

For any crisis situation, here is a sample outline for a response. Use this as a starting point to craft your crisis communication and message response strategy. This needs to be communicated internally as well—during times of crisis it's not just the public that is affected; your employees are, too. Your response needs to demonstrate that you've humanized the experience as much as possible—meaning that you care about more than the bottom line and how the situation is impacting it.

13 / When the Sh*t Hits the Fan

Step One: Own Your Sh*t

Take responsibility and apologize to all involved. State the most pertinent facts at the outset.

Step Two: Address the Needs

Alleviate any immediate questions or what's on the top of people's minds.

Step Three: Sympathize and Empathize

Share genuine empathy and connection—demonstrate you know what's at stake.

Step Four: Report the Solution

State what you're doing as an ongoing effort to right the wrong or fix the problem.

Step Five: Apologize, Again

Apologize again to all involved. Thank parties as appropriate.

We respond to the human condition. Mistakes happen. How you handle those mistakes will determine the aftermath of the crisis.

Ongoing Situation Maintenance

As a crisis unfolds, and even as it draws to an end, continual updating and monitoring of all communication channels is key. Even if there is nothing new to report, err on the side of caution and post frequent updates. We live in a time where access to information is expected and instant gratification is the status quo. The last thing you want is to have information buried when customers and employees are looking for immediate answers.

Make it easy for people to find relevant information. "Pin" a post at the top of your social media feeds so users don't have to scroll for information. Create a pop-up that loads immediately on your website highlighting the important details and paths of action. Put a temporary header on your website alerting people to the situation and what can be done to meet their needs. Communicate response times and expectations as clearly as possible.

Update on facts. What you know. What you're doing. Always apologize to your multiple audiences, and mean it. Not just in a "sorry you're inconvenienced" way, but in a way that lets your customers know that you really understand the situation they're in and the frustration they're experiencing.

One of the best ongoing crisis responses I've seen happened in July 2016, when Southwest Airlines experienced a systemwide outage that impacted more than 250,000 travelers. Here are the first few lines of a response from Southwest Airline's Chief Operating Officer that will likely go down in textbooks of the future as a gold-star response.

First of all I want to apologize to our customers and our employees. I realize how frustrating it can be to have your travel plans disrupted and I realize that some of those travel plans are for some really special moments that can't be replaced, so I want to thank our employees for their heroic efforts and also our customers for their incredible patience.

He then went on to detail the process, the solutions that were being worked on, and again thanked and apologized.

Notice that his response contains the first three elements in the general outline provided earlier. And he did so in a genuine, authentic, and empathetic way.

For example, after the Southwest Airlines system outage, angry customers across the country were shouting out via social media. But, empowered to do whatever was in the best interest of the customer, employees at airports made attempts to provide as much comfort as possible in the middle of a major travel crisis. Just as angry tweets filled the company's feeds, so did positive images of gate areas with Southwest employees delivering and serving pizza, communicating the facts of the situation to stranded passengers, and doing everything in their power to help remedy travel plans.

No matter what, in all your communications, be authentic and genuine. If you want to see the difference authenticity makes, check out the contrast between Southwest Airlines' and Delta's video-based responses to their respective technical outages in July and August 2016.

If you want to understand the difference that empathetic and genuine delivery can make during a crisis situation, look no further than these two examples.

In July and August 2016, two major airlines—Southwest and Delta—experienced technical outages that stranded or disrupted the travel of hundreds of thousands of passengers. This caused travelers to miss important meetings, life experiences, and business opportunities. At the very least, for nonessential travel, it created a lot of frustration and stress.

Both airlines used video to address the crisis. But they did so in very different ways.

Southwest Response

Southwest went live. They used Facebook livestream to reach their audience directly, instead of issuing reports through traditional media. Each stream was done within Southwest headquarters and had employees working in the background. This was not a traditional corporate video. The people on camera were in polo shirts or polo shirts with a jacket, not a corporate suit and tie. While an outline was followed, you can tell a lot of the responses were non-prepped, off the cuff, and vulnerable. Midcrisis, during the second livestream (Southwest did a total of three; this one lasted 6:35), they streamed from the Listening Center, bringing in the COO and showing employees at work. Someone from the social business team also got on the stream to talk about communication and how to resolve travel problems. There was an apology to both customers and employees. A human connection. Statements of facts and solutions in progress. A visual display of those solutions in progress. And another apology. Overall, a solid response that got favorable results.

Delta Response

Delta posted a 58-second video of its CEO giving an update during the crisis. He did a good job stating the facts, but it's very clear he's reading off a script (and, since the video wasn't live, we don't know how many takes he needed—it could just be one, but we'll never know). They took a page from the Southwest stream and recorded the video in their offices where employees were working frantically in the background. That was a smart move. But the CEO is in a suit and tie, very poised, and delivering a script. When you speak from a script, it's very difficult to demonstrate empathy, as your paralanguage won't vary as easily (more on that in the next chapter). Another big difference was there was never an apology to the employees. Their hard work was noted and they received a thank-you, but the apology was just to the customers. There wasn't much of a connection made to the viewer. Today, this is the epitome of corporate video—even five years ago this would've been ahead of the curve. It no longer is.

Remember, communication is more than words. Delivery of those words is important, too. When it comes to a crisis, it's not just what you say or how you say it—it's the combination of what you say, how you say it, and the actions that follow that will determine how the image of the business is remembered and restored.

⊙ ⊙ ⊙

In the next chapter, we'll go into delivery skills for public speaking. That chapter provides tips that touch on many different areas of communication in the workplace and beyond, including tips that can be used to deliver crisis responses.

Speak Out, Speak Up

Giving Presentations That Inspire Action

14

How to Not Suck on Stage

Delivery Skills for Public Speaking

I don't know a single person, even a seasoned professional speaker, who doesn't get at least a few nervous butterflies before they speak. Because when you care, you want to do a good job. When you want to do well, that amps you up and changes your body chemistry, and you get anxious. I tell myself that the first time I walk on stage and don't feel any anxiety, I shouldn't be presenting that day.

But I'm also aware there's a big difference between a few excited butterflies and paralyzing fear. Studies show that one of the best ways to ease public-speaking anxiety is to engage in visualization exercises, where you envision yourself speaking and succeeding. We won't get into visualization techniques in this chapter, as that is not in my wheelhouse. However, we will get into some of the main areas of delivery and strategy and provide exercises you can do to practice and improve, so you can better visualize and realize your speaking success.

When it comes to giving a great public speech or presentation, it's not just what you say or how you say it but the combination of those two things, along with the experience you provide and the feeling you leave with your audience, that creates results. This chapter focuses on the "how" and experience portions. The following chapter dives into the "what" and feelings aspects.

Stop Boxing Yourself In

The first time I ever gave a public speech, I was 9 years old (it was at a local 4-H club in a small town in Kansas). While I vaguely remember the setting and the feeling of nervousness, what I remember clearly is walking slowly up to the easel and delivering my opening line, swiveling my head dramatically around the room with each pause: "Hello (pause) my name is Jill (pause) Schiefelbein (pause) and my topic is (pause) how (pause) to draw (pause) a mouse (pause)."

Really. You can't make this stuff up.

While I over-corrected in slowing down my speech for the introduction, as soon as I started I got so excited and nervous that I zoomed through the presentation like an auctioneer, leaving time to spare. See, I forgot to do two things—get the pre-speech jitters physically out of my body and, quite frankly, breathe.

Later in my public-speaking journey I still struggled with the whole breathing thing. I'd get so excited and speak so quickly that in the middle of a presentation I'd practically have to gasp for air before moving on to the next point. To this day I still have a tendency to speak quickly, but I've now found a way to channel it into the energy and flow of my presentations instead of having an awkward moment of inhalation.

I tell you this story not only to poke fun at myself—which I'll willingly do—but to also show you that I discovered my delivery tendencies and found a way to make them work for me.

If you put me up against a column of "what makes a good public speaker" characteristics in a standard public-speaking textbook, I wouldn't measure up. But what those textbooks don't account for is the experiences and feelings that authentic, flawed, vulnerable delivery provides for an audience. I pay my bills by speaking to audiences small and large. And I've gotten comfortable with my imperfections to the point where I've made them work for me.

You can do the same thing. Quit putting yourself in a box. Quit comparing yourself to what others are like as speakers. They are not you. The key is to find out your own strengths and weaknesses so you can craft a delivery style that emphasizes your strengths and repositions your so-called weaknesses.

I speak quickly. Instead of saying "Stop that, you need to slow down," I decided to find a way to channel that speed into my delivery. I focused on variation in rate and intentional repetition, choosing to work my fast-talking tendencies into the presentation instead of ignoring them. This helped me craft a delivery style that is all my own.

Now that you're going to stop comparing yourself to others and start working on your own unique style, let's look at five different categories of delivery skills that you can incorporate into your public-speaking persona.

REAL PEOPLE, REAL STORIES, REAL RESULTS

Kat Loterzo

CEO and Founder, Kat Loterzo

Entrepreneurship Is Anything but Linear

It's all over the place. There's really no point in trying to put together a pretty plan. You need to know what the big picture is, what the vision is, and what you ultimately want to create. As soon as you start putting your focus into figuring out the perfect plan, you're taking your eye off that vision, and you're focusing instead on the steps. Know what you need to do now, and do it.

Being an Entrepreneur Is About Learning to Enjoy the Chaos

If you're a natural-born entrepreneur, you'll never be content and never be satisfied. You will never feel that you did enough. You'll never complete your task list. You're going to die, and it still won't be done, so just come to terms with it now and enjoy the chaos. It's not about if you're this organized person who does everything in a finite, predetermined, categorized way, day-by-day, and is really structured. If you were, you wouldn't be an entrepreneur! Embrace who you are.

Trying to Be "Perfect" Is Exhausting

When I first started speaking, I remember feeling so much pressure to do things perfectly. I would spend ages trying to create fancy slide shows and worry extensively about being professional enough, and good enough, and making sure I presented myself in a certain way. I stressed about what people would think. I found it pretty tiring. Now, I just let out what is inside me and trust myself.

There's Really Nothing You Can Do That Will Kill You on Stage

I think one of the things that's toughest for speakers starting out is fear of screwing up. Realize that if you forget where you're at, or if you say something silly or embarrassing, or if you make a mistake, or even if you totally fall off the edge of the stage, it's fine. You can just keep going. There's really nothing you can do that will kill you on stage.

Be Unapologetically You

For anybody who wants to market online or offline, if you're not willing to be unapologetic about what you stand for, what you stand against, and who you're here to serve, nobody will ever see or notice you because you will not stand out. Your ideal clients will never know you're there. You have to go all-in at being you.

The Biggest Mistake Is Not Speaking Your Truth

The one thing I wish I would have learned earlier, if I could go back ten years and give myself advice, would be to just be authentically you and screw the rest. Stop trying to be someone you're not. You're just never going to be satisfied if you don't be who you truly are in your business. I also fully believe that you'll never create wealth or true impact if you don't fully believe in and speak your truth.

Eye Contact

Eye contact is the number-one conveyor of honesty in the United States. It's said the eyes are the windows to the soul (gag), but when it comes down to it, we don't trust people when we can't see their eyes. Ever zoomed past an online dating profile because every picture had sunglasses? Me, too. What are you hiding?!

When it comes to public speaking, though, making and maintaining eye contact can be tough. Looking at a piece of paper is so much easier. You know why? Because the paper doesn't have eyeballs staring back at you. The paper doesn't judge.

But here's the truth: You have no clue what your audience is thinking. Really.

And if you think you do, get off your ego trip and come back down to reality.

Of course we'd like to think that by making eye contact with our audience we have captivated the entire room. The reality is, though, that someone may be looking at you but thinking about the doughnut in the break room (or maybe that's just me—I do love doughnuts).

If you're scared of making eye contact, I get it. Really. But you need to do it. If it makes you nervous, here are some exercises to try until you can get it right.

Look at the top of the heads of people in your audience. Some say look at the shoes, but honestly, if you do that, you may end up looking at something that can get you in a lot of trouble. Don't do that! Make "eye contact" by scanning the top of heads in the room. If you have a room of 25 plus, the only people who will realize you're not making direct eye contact with them are the person you're looking at and potentially the ones next to him.

Next, graduate to the forehead. You're so close now! Get comfortable with the forehead and then make your way slowly to the eyes. It's systematic desensitization. If you feel you're an eye contact pro, watch yourself on video and see what side of the room you tend to favor more. Note that, and gradually start to adjust to even it out.

Enunciation and Pronunciation

How you articulate and pronounce words is important because people need to be able to understand you. Duh. But if you get a little anxious or nervous, or are naturally excitable like I am, you tend to speak fast. And then faster and faster, until pretty soon you're an auctioneer. At that point you're not enunciating well and your clarity is going to suffer.

Your audience won't catch everything you're saying. You'll lack maximum effectiveness. You won't be dynamic.

Boo.

Here are some ways to help with your enunciation and pronunciation. First, show your teeth!

Seriously.

I'm about as musically inclined as a rock plopping in a lake. That's not an exaggeration. In fact, I should probably start a GoFundMe to get myself vocal lessons. I'm so bad that people would probably pitch in (bad pun intended).

Despite my inability to carry a tune, I did learn two things in my elementary school music class that are incredibly useful when it comes to public speaking and effective delivery.

The first is that to enunciate, you need to show your teeth. The best lip sync performers are so believable because as they mouth the words, their teeth are showing. Watch your favorite singers—the ones belting out tunes I can only dream of. Their pearly whites are showing. Because in order to get that type of sound out, the mouth needs to be open and the air pipes clear. So if you find yourself starting to speak too quickly, think about showing some of your teeth (in other words, open your mouth a little wider). If you're not sure whether you do this, watch yourself speak in a mirror. Better yet, set up a camera and record yourself in conversation or during a video chat. You'll be able to see your tendencies that way.

The second musical lesson I learned has to do with pronunciation. The singers and artists that have lyrics you can actually understand and sing along with have something in common—they pronounce the consonants clearly, especially the final consonant of each word.

Try it. Say "world" out loud without focusing on the final "d" in your pronunciation. Now say it while pronouncing the last "d" clearly. Practice this in your head (or even better, out loud) with other words. You'll notice it makes a difference.

Another thing: Don't put words in your speech that you can't or don't know how to pronounce! And if you make a mistake, laugh, own it, and move on.

Paralanguage

Paralanguage is everything other than the words in your speech. It's your rate, tone, and pitch. The rate is the speed at which you speak. The tone is the relative volume of your voice—are you loud or soft? The pitch is the natural highness or lowness of your voice—think high notes and low notes.

The three combined convey emotion, confidence, and power during a presentation.

Effective paralanguage is like a vocal roller coaster. In a good amusement park ride, you have highs and lows, twists and turns, loops and straights. So, too, should a good speech have variation in rate, tone, and pitch.

As an aside, paralanguage is what a lot of human lie detectors use to tell if someone is lying or fudging the truth. If you play the game Two Truths and a Lie, in which people make three statements—two are true and one is false—a trained listener will detect slight differences in paralanguage with the lie (at least for most nonsociopathic people). Try it with your friends. It's a fun party game.

As mentioned multiple times already in this book, actions speak louder than words. This means that your actions and your words must be synonymous; so should your words and your paralanguage. For example, you don't want to use a high pitch and fast rate of speech if you are delivering a serious message with lots of detail. Likewise, you don't want to speak in a low tone and slow voice if you're trying to convey excitement and happiness.

Nobody likes to listen to a monotonous speaker. You know that person who stands unmoving behind the podium, speaking at a flat level the entire time (think Ben Stein's voice for an entire speech, except replace Ben Stein with a business owner or salesperson). Yikes!

Speaking of podiums, let's talk about them and why they sometimes aren't a good idea.

SPOILER ALERT

We'll look at different forms of nonverbal barriers and how they impact delivery and buy-in in Chapters 16 and 21.

Nonverbal Barriers

The use of space in your presentation is important. Most people take a presentation space at face value—that what they see is what they get— or they walk into a room, see a podium, and immediately gravitate there.

Don't do that right away!

Evaluate the space to see what type of barrier you might be placing between yourself and your audience, and how you might be better able to use the space to your advantage. Learn from this story as to why this is so important.

When I taught business communication, one of the capstone projects my students did was an organizational communication audit. They were to come as a small group and present the findings and recommendations to a mock board of directors (myself and two businesspeople I brought in as volunteer graders). The presentation was done in a small conference room with 12 chairs. Student groups were three to four people. Upon the students entering the room, the judging panel stood to shake hands and then sat down. Without fail, every single student group did one thing that would've likely cost them business on the spot—they stood the entire time.

Standing during a presentation is a power play. And if you want to earn my business, standing over me and "telling" me information is not the way to do it.

After they gave the presentations, I invited the students to sit down and asked, "How do you feel now that you're sitting down?"

"Much better, less awkward, more relaxed," were the common replies. *"Why didn't you sit down to give the presentation?"* I asked. *"Because it's a presentation. You're supposed to stand up,"* they said.

"Says who?"

A presentation doesn't have to be made standing up. In fact, in some situations—like this one—it would hurt your delivery. Assess the room and the environment. Figure out how to best connect with your audience and deliver from a point of connection, not a point of power. Don't put unnecessary nonverbal barriers between you and your audience.

Gestures and Movement

With the exception of a few extraordinary speakers, most presenters don't do their best standing perfectly still. It's hard to convey emotion if your body is rigidly standing in a single position. Alas, sometimes you have to use a podium, limiting your movement. Here's what you can do.

If you have to use a podium, you can still use gestures! Just make sure they are done above the waist. Do them with intent, power, and confidence. Make them visible to your audience. And as you gesture, lean forward slightly. You may also lean forward to emphasize a point or increase connection.

Make sure your gestures and words are synonymous. If you're enumerating a list and adding gestures, make sure the numbers you're saying match the number of fingers you're holding up (and, of course, be conscious what finger you're holding up!). Even without a podium, keeping your gestures above the waist is a good rule of thumb.

If you can move around the room or stage, be sure your movements are intentional. Don't move just for the sake of moving. Instead, move to transition between points or stories or characters. And don't let your movements be a way for nervous energy to escape your body. Don't be a pacer, a hula dancer, a weight shifter, or a toe tapper. Move and gesture when it is natural and purposeful. And if it's not natural to you at this point, don't stress about it. Work on one thing at a time until you craft your own unique style.

Quick Practice Tips

The best way to improve on your public speaking is to get out there and do it! Then get it on video so you can review your delivery style.

To practice before a presentation, first record your presentation with just audio. Pay attention to the paralanguage and the enunciation and pronunciation. Also note the feeling. Does your voice elicit emotion? If not, focus on improving that.

Second, record a practice presentation with video. Then watch that video on mute. This will make you keenly aware of your body movements and gestures. You'll be able to observe if you favor one side of the room or another with your eyes and body posturing.

Finally, watch the video with the sound on. This is where you bring it all together. It's best to isolate the delivery variables to determine where you need to improve. After a presentation, use the same video strategy, watching on mute first, then with full sound.

⊙ ⊙ ⊙

In the next chapter, we'll expand on presentation skills by going into organizational patterns. This chapter covered the physical delivery skills. The next chapter will cover the content.

Structure Is Sexy

Organizing Presentation Materials and Speeches

While the delivery aspects of public speaking are incredibly important, so too is the organization of your content and material. Remember, dynamic communication is the combination of verbal and nonverbal, the experience and feelings, and the results that follow. This chapter provides a strategy for organizing your content for presentations of all types (formal public speeches, speeches at industry events, informative presentations, etc.). We start with unveiling the elements of effective introductions and conclusions and then provide a basic organizational structure for any speech, paper, presentation, or briefing. We'll end with different types of organizational patterns you can use to present your information in a clear, compelling way.

Some of what you'll see in this chapter might give you flashbacks to a speech or English class you had in school. While I'm sorry for any traumatic memories this chapter may conjure up, I don't apologize for presenting this information, because so many speeches I hear are terribly unorganized and leave the audience confused and frustrated. Follow the advice here, and your presentation won't be one of those! Let's start at the beginning.

Introductions

I believe the best speeches come full circle. That means the introduction and conclusion tie back together in some way, leaving the audience with a feeling of completion. If you tell a story at the beginning, you tie it back together at the end. If you tell a joke at the beginning, you reference it somehow at the end. You get the picture.

Your introduction should always contain three parts. The first part is where you gain the audience's attention, often called the attention-getter. In public-speaking classes you're often encouraged to use an anecdote, a joke, some other form of humor, a startling statistic, or a quotation. Those can all work just fine, but whatever you do, make sure your opening line is directly related to your audience and the purpose for the presentation.

The second part of your introduction is the purpose statement. Basically, this is you stating why you are there to present information. This may seem obvious to some, but stating this right out helps reduce uncertainty and establishes expectations—two strategies you've already learned about in this book.

Finally, a good introduction will have a preview statement. This indicates what is to come during the presentation. You can think of this as a presentation agenda, letting your audience know what it's in for. A typical format is: "I'll start off by [sharing] X. Next, we'll [uncover] Y. Finally, we'll [look at possible solutions for] Z." (Insert whatever verbs are relative to your content and purpose.)

Having these three elements in your introduction reduces uncertainty, sets a stage for success, and establishes clear expectations, not only about what you will deliver but also what the audience should mentally prepare for.

It is also important to set the parameters for interaction. For example, are you going to accept questions during the presentation, or would you like people to hold them until the end? How would you like your audience to listen? What would you like them to keep in mind while you are presenting your materials? Would you like them to think through the process? These are all things to think about and communicate in a good introduction.

Did you notice I used this model in writing the introduction to this chapter? You can use these organizational strategies for written communication, too!

Opening attention-getter:

While the delivery aspects of public speaking are incredibly import-ant, so is the organization of your content and material. Remember, dynamic communication is the combination of verbal and nonverbal, the experience and feelings, and the results that follow.

Purpose statement:

This chapter provides a strategy for organizing your content for presentations of all types (formal public speeches, speeches at industry events, informative presentations, etc.).

Preview of the main points:

We start with unveiling the elements of effective introductions and conclusions and then provide a basic organizational structure for any speech, paper, presentation, or briefing. We'll end with different types of organizational patterns you can use to present your informa-tion in a clear, compelling way.

Conclusions

Your conclusion, like your introduction, has three parts. The first part is a summary of your main points. This follows the popular philosophy "tell them what you're going to tell them, tell them, then tell them what you told them." This is also a chance to emphasize the most important points of the presentation that you want to ensure people remember.

The second part of the conclusion is to remind people of your purpose. This is where the conclusion starts to come full circle and refer back to the introduction. You don't need to state it in exactly the same language, but referencing it again is important. It reminds people why they are in the room, and sometimes what action you want them to take.

Finally, you want to tie it all together and make your request. This is your final chance to deliver a solid one-two punch. The best conclusions in this instance will refer back to the attention-getter in the introduction and put it all together for the audience. And you don't want to forget one of the most overlooked parts—telling the audience what you want them to do with the information.

This is so important that I need to state it again: You need to tell your audience what to *do* with the information you provided. What action do they need to take? What is the next step? Leaving this out is one of the biggest and most common mistakes people make.

Now that you know how to start and finish the organization of your content, let's dive into the main body of your presentation and learn some cool organization tips.

REAL PEOPLE, REAL STORIES, REAL RESULTS

Robin Koval

CEO and President, Truth Initiative, *New York Times* and *Wall Street Journal* Bestselling Co-Author

Create the Kind of Advertising That Becomes Part of Culture

The most effective and persuasive kinds of communication are not built by simply telling people your side of the story and trying to change their minds. Instead, it's about identifying a meaningful insight and presenting it in a different, and surprising way. It's imperative to offer a cultural truth that is unique from the other white noise out there–a truth that is relatable and thought provoking. This gets heads nodding, and people taking ownership of an idea, ultimately leading to action. That creates pop culture. That creates change.

Marry Facts with Cultural Relevancy to Drive Change

When you can take facts and marry them up with something that's culturally relevant, you've created a reason to get people to pay attention to you. What's incredibly interesting to us as marketers is not always that interesting to consumers.

As we develop our campaign strategies, we take the posture that our young customers don't care much about the issue of tobacco. For example, we know that while young people know the health consequences of smoking, they don't connect with that information on an emotional level since health effects don't matter to them right now. We have to think, "What do young people really care about?" They care about relationships. They care about social justice issues. They care about animal welfare. In order to be relevant and heard by young people, we tether the issue of smoking in our campaigns to things that are meaningful to them in the here and now. That gives us the chance to capture people's attention in an emotionally relevant way.

Stop Trying to Make Your Messages Do Too Much

Sometimes the mistake that gets made is trying to do too much or over complicate the message. If you can't make your story simple—able to be captured in a single sentence or in your elevator speech—then the consumer is going to lose interest and not pay attention to you. Sometimes marketers fall into the trap of thinking that their messages will resonate if they can get customers to listen long and hard enough. But that doesn't work. When you think about the key elements of successful campaigns, it's the simple ideas that stick.

Put Your Head on the Customer's Shoulders

We tend to get very focused on our own goals—whether that's a sales objective, a bottom line number or, in our case, our intention to keep young people from smoking. But success lies in turning the telescope around and thinking about the value that you bring to your target audience. In our case, teenagers have a lot of things competing for their attention, so there's always a value proposition that you need to create. At the end of the day, it's about them, it's not about you.

Main Content Organizational Patterns

The basic organization of any presentation, speech, or paper can be looked at as a series of main points and subpoints.

You can use a simple "main and supporting point" organizational style, where your supporting points are pieces of information necessary for your audience to understand your main point or data that supports your claim. Think, "If I want someone to do X, they need to understand Y," or, "If I want someone to remember X, I need to contextualize it with Y." Figure 15–1 is a sample outline you can use to help you.

Within your main points you can organize your content in one of three ways: chronologically, topically, or spatially.

1. *Chronological organization* is based on time. First, second, third. Or reverse order. When you're presenting the status of a project, often a chronological organization makes the most sense. When you're presenting the history of something, this is likely a good choice.

2. *Topical organization* is based on—you guessed it—topic. If you're doing an all-hands meeting and are updating on the status of each department, each department would be a topic in the presentation (which you then tie together with your introduction and conclusion, ideally in a way that motivates, boosts morale, and ultimately increases productivity). You can also organize topically by questions, which is a good strategy that my friend Andy Crestodina of Orbit Media uses. He divides his main presentation points by questions that will be answered—smart!

3. *Spatial organization* is based on physical space or geography or user experience. If you're doing a product demonstration, for example, it will likely make sense to start the audience out on the same journey they would go on as the user of a product. Similarly, if you were giving instructions on how to get somewhere, you'd use this pattern.

No matter which pattern you use, it's important to give your audience a structure so your presentation and information are not lost in translation. You want to also make sure to transition from one point

Basic Presentation Organization Outline

Introduction

1. Get attention

2. State purpose

3. Preview main points

Main Presentation Body

1. First main point

   A. Supporting point

   B. Supporting point

2. Second main point

   A. Supporting point

   B. Supporting point

3. Third main point

   A. Supporting point

   B. Supporting point

Conclusion

1. Summarize main points

2. Reiterate purpose

3. Tie together and call to act

FIGURE 15–1

Basic Presentation Organization Outline

to another smoothly. The simple way to think about this is: "We just talked about X, now we're going to move on to Y." I encourage you to be more creative than that, but you are essentially posting verbal signs to your audience to tell them you're transitioning from one area to the next. Here are a couple more examples: "You just learned how to do X.

Now, let's see how that enables you to do Y." "We just discussed the reasons against X. But there are also some positive aspects to unveil." Not surprisingly, in communication these transitions are often called signposts.

⊙ ⊙ ⊙

In the next chapter, we'll shift the focus to persuasion. The last two chapters were really focused on basic delivery and organization for information-based presentations. The next two chapters dive into specific delivery considerations and content strategies for persuasive communication.

CHAPTER

16

Get People to Act

Persuasion and Hugging with Words

I t can be argued that every act of intentional communication is an attempt to persuade. At the very least, when you communicate you want people to believe you are credible and worth listening to. In business, most communication is persuasive in some way. Knowing this, and knowing you want to drive action in and grow your business, it's important to understand some delivery aspects of persuasive speech and how you can use them to be more effective.

Ethos, Pathos, Logos

Flash back to your high school English class or a college speech course. You probably were introduced to these three tenets of rhetoric at some point. Or, as Aristotle called them, the three artistic proofs. Now, let's put them in context for what they really mean when it comes to dynamic communication and driving results and action in your business.

1. Ethos is credibility.
2. Pathos is emotion.
3. Logos is logic.

The combination of these three elements in any presentation will increase the likelihood of driving action.

Ethos

When it comes to establishing credibility, many business owners, especially successful ones, are tempted to rest on their laurels. In today's information-heavy economy, the consumer has more choices than ever before, and more avenues for information access than have ever existed. Your digital footprint provides part of the initial communication history and communicates your ethos to an audience. During a formal presentation, this can also come in the form of your introduction. Ethos may also be scattered throughout your presentation by using anecdotes and case studies, or by referencing projects that demonstrate your expertise or ability to produce positive change.

FLASHBACK

Communication history, your digital footprint, and how the information economy and how it changes the way we need to communicate to be effective are covered in the Introduction and Chapter 1.

Pathos

Pathos, or the emotional connection with your audience, comes from cultivating feelings of connection, safety, and accessibility. People with whom you make a human connection are more likely to be invested in what you have to say. Those who bank on a fear-based approach will establish some amount of pathos, as fear does evoke emotion. This may work as a one-off, but if you want sustained results and action, you need to establish a positive emotional connection with your audience. I'll go into this in more detail later in this chapter with specific strategies on how you can accomplish the emotional connection.

Logos

Logos is an appeal based on logic. It is where a lot of people start off in the sales conversation. We start out with the features of, or information about, our products or services. We want to get the sale, but we are so focused on telling about all the great things our product or service can do that we fail to make the emotional connection with the audience. And, in doing so often fail to establish the initial credibility. While logical appeals are incredibly important to persuasion, especially in business environments, alone they are typically not enough to drive sustained action. Even the most logical thinker has an emotional desire somewhere to be more efficient, impact change, or make a condition better. That's why ethos, pathos, and logos are grouped together as this triad.

Now that you understand the different appeals that need to be present in any persuasive communicative effort, let's look deeper into how you can manifest these appeals through your presentations.

REAL PEOPLE, REAL STORIES, REAL RESULTS

Christophe Pienkowski

Senior Brand Ambassador, Martell

Leveraging Your Brand Through Ambassadors

Your ambassadors can come from anywhere inside or outside your organization. I started as a chef. Through hosting pairing dinners, I found I enjoyed talking with the customers. I was so passionate about food and pairing it with our product. Passion is essential. Think of who in your organization is doing a role that may not be customer facing right now that could be customer facing and relate in a way that a salesperson couldn't.

Your Brand Ambassadors Are the People People

My advice for brand ambassadors? Of course you need to like your brand, but you also need to like people. That's one of the most important things. I used to travel a lot, for

---

example, in Asia. You go in those places and you arrive at the beginning of the evening and nobody is smiling, everybody is very serious. At the end of the night, you are best friends. That's something very personal. You have to really feel people. You have to love people in general, and to be able, of course, to share your passion for your brand. That's the most important thing.

Leveraging Your Brand Through Partnerships

When we launched a new cognac expression, we looked at the product, its development, its roots, and its connection to other elements of life. As a brand we've always been linked to the world of art. Creating a new product is a highly creative and innovative process. What other industries are creative and innovative? We partnered with artists, with deejays, with digital photographers, with culinary innovators to make the launch a more well-rounded experience with partners that complement our brand, bringing together creativity and passion.

Great Brand Experiences Tell a Story

It's important for people to understand the story behind a brand or a product, to find a way to get emotionally connected to it. For us, it's very important for the people to see where we actually make Martell expressions. During our product launch, attendees were able to see the vineyards, the hills, the factories, all the intimate images of how this product was created, and the story was told through those pictures.

When You Are an Ambassador, Relive the Experience Every Time

Great brand ambassadors remember what it's like to experience your product or service for the first time. It's like reliving the experience every time, putting yourselves in the shoes of the person or people you're speaking with. And then there's the joy of getting to watch someone interact with, or in my case taste, your product for the first time. It's incredible.

Time to TEMPTaction

Here is a five-step model I call the TEMPTaction model. It's created based on an understanding of persuasion, great public-speaking delivery, and communication principles. You won't find it in any textbooks, but you will find it executed in effective presentations. Let's take a deeper look.

Touch

The first "T" in TEMPTaction stands for *touch*. This doesn't mean you need to physically reach out and touch your customers, and in some cases that might get you in trouble. It means you need to metaphorically touch them with your communication. People make decisions based on emotion. If there is no emotional connection, they are not likely to act. If they do not see your reasoning or a need to act, people won't decide. It is important to establish this human touch in all your communication, both in-person and virtually.

Another way to think of touch is to think of hugging people with your words. You need to communicate in a way that makes people feel embraced by your message. They need to feel engaged listening to you, they need to trust you, and they need to be able to take comfort in what you're saying.

FLASHBACK

Common communication denominators are discussed in Chapter 10; they give you ways to use language to more effectively connect with your audience and get everyone on the same page. See how these concepts are all tying together?

When people are relaxed and not on guard, they're more likely to be open to your messaging and your requests for action.

This metaphorical idea of touch is often best demonstrated by tying in analogies, metaphors, and storytelling, and by making a direct connection to a person's life or situation. And the bigger your audience is, the more important it is to think of the common communication denominators. This way you're letting each audience member decide for herself how to relate to your content, and she can pull in an experience from her life to make that connection. Let me share a story about a persuasive conversation that made a meaningful connection to me (and my bank account).

I've talked to a handful of financial planners in my life, and the one I chose, even though he's now on the opposite side of the country and my situation has changed since we originally started working together, is the person who sat me down in a room and said, "Jill, what does money mean to you?"

"What do you mean?" I asked.

"Let's pretend you had all the money you needed to take care of all your bills, pay off the house, pay your health expenses, etc. Let's say you didn't have to stress about money in this way. What does money mean to you?"

With my response, we started a conversation about how I like to give back to the community, my philanthropic activities, and projects I would like to do that money would allow me to execute. We talked about how I want to travel more and take at least one longer international vacation each year.

Unlike other planners I'd spoken to, he didn't have me look at money in the past or money in the future—in terms of where I'd like to end up during retirement, or what I need to leave behind after death (not such a pleasant thought). Instead, he first wanted to get a solid understanding of what money meant to me in my life. He made a personal and emotional connection.

From that, he was able to assess my values. Based on those values, he prescribed what he thought was the appropriate amount of risks for my investments, etc., which is what a financial planner does. But he did it with my personal goals in mind.

What he did that caught my attention was make it personal. He demonstrated that he really cared about what money enables me to do in my life. Instead of simply saying, "What number do you want to reach?", he positioned the goal in a different way: "Let's say you reach that number: What is that going to look like, and how is that going to manifest in your life?" That was much more personal than, "Oh, we'll get you to a million dollars by the time you're 40."

Instead, he focused on the value it would bring, the benefits and results that would come from reaching a monetary goal. He positioned it as "Here's what it's going to enable you to do," and that was more important for me.

That is a prime example of hugging with words, and of providing the metaphorical touch in a persuasive presentation or conversation.

Eye Contact

The "E" in TEMPTaction stands for *eye contact*. As we already know from Chapter 14, eye contact is the number-one conveyor of honesty in the United States. If you're going to persuade somebody to act, you have to establish a comfortable rapport with your eyes. If somebody does not trust you, or feels you are being dishonest, they are not going to act, decide, or buy. If you're communicating via video, natural eye contact is also important.

> **FLASHBACK**
>
> In Chapter 9, I shared a very humbling story with you about the first time I focused on making eye contact on a video. There are also a handful of video delivery tips included that will help you be better on camera.

Movement

The "M" stands for *movement*. You need to incorporate movement into your speech or presentation if you want to persuade people. Movement is not only about the physical space and positioning of the body, but also the idea of moving people from one point to another. You must demonstrate that your product or service can move someone from their current position to a better position. When your request has that capability to move someone to a better position, or change the status quo in a positive way, it is more likely to produce an action. If you have already established a solid sense of touch, this movement will be more about the information and executory practices of your proposal.

In a physical sense, when it comes to your delivery, movement means you are transitioning your body through space with a purpose.

You're not interacting with slides or other presentation tools. You have eliminated nonverbal barriers, such as podiums, conference tables, or inappropriate use of power stance (like standing to give a presentation when there are only five other people in the room). You are using movement to transition your audience from point

> **SPOILER ALERT**
>
> In Chapter 17, we're going to discuss a specific framework for organizing your messages to cater to a persuasive presentation.

to point. Your stance shifts in major transitions. You use your body to gesture and indicate different aspects of the presentation. Your movements have a purpose, and are not just flighty, twitchy, or nervous jitters.

Paralanguage

The "P" stands for *paralanguage*. As you know from Chapter 14, this is everything other than your words and presentation. This is your rate, tone, and pitch. If you need a refresher: The rate is the speed at which you speak. The tone is the relative volume of your voice—are you loud or soft? The pitch is the natural highness or lowness of your voice—think high notes and low notes.

Turning back to the psychology of decision making, people need to feel an emotional connection between you, your product, and their situation in order to act. If you want to drive people to action and your business, which I assume you do if you're reading this book, you need to make sure your voice conveys emotion. This also applies to text-based communication.

> *Go back more than a decade (yikes, I feel old), to when I did my graduate research on how people expressed nonverbal communication and paralanguage in written messages online. It was one of the first works published about the use of signifiers in online and computer-mediated communication. The idea that one could nonverbally communicate without being visually or auditorially present was rejected by many academics at the time.*

I argued that paralanguage, in terms of written messaging, is demonstrated with the use of signifiers and emoticons (those things we now call emojis). Signifiers are the changes you make to text, such as boldface, italics, bulleted lists, and appropriate use of white space. The use of these communicates nonverbally through text.

See? These persuasive strategies can apply to any communication— written or spoken.

Training

The final "T" stands for *training*. This is where you practice your delivery, get feedback from relevant audiences, and implement that feedback and change into your next iteration. This is also where you use activities to practice your presentation, such as the audio and video recording techniques we talked about in Chapter 14.

Training, when it comes to persuasive communication, also involves gathering data on the success of your presentations and conversion rates. Did you get the actions you intended?

⊙　⊙　⊙

In the next chapter, we'll learn one of the most effective frameworks for organizing persuasive messages. This takes what we learned in Chapter 15 to the next level and helps you better drive actions, decisions, and results.

CHAPTER

17

The Organized Mind Buys

Sequencing Content for Persuasive Impact

The organizational patterns presented in Chapter 15 are a solid foundation for categorizing and presenting information. But if your goal is persuasion, I want to introduce you to my favorite organizational structure for any presentation given for the purpose of driving action. In fact, I use it to help me mentally plan almost all my business communication. I wish I could take credit for creating it, but, alas, I cannot. It's called Monroe's Motivated Sequence.

If you've heard of it before, you may be having flashbacks to your college days, where you learned it in a public-speaking class. But I'm guessing, if you're like I was as a student, you memorized what you needed to know for a test and haven't done much with it since. The real-life tests in business are not about how many terms you can pull up from memory, but rather how persuasive you are and what actions you can elicit. Remember earlier when I said that knowledge is information applied? Let's learn how to apply this information to help you grow, lead, and manage your business.

Allow me to introduce Monroe's Motivated Sequence, and then tell you how to actually apply it to make positive changes, deliver presentations that will be remembered, and drive results. Note that this is not just an organizational sequence for large public speeches or presentations; it can also be used as an organizational framework for any business conversation. Let me geek out for a minute and tell you the story about how the framework originated.

In the mid-1930s, a Purdue University professor named Alan H. Monroe decided (and I'm paraphrasing here), "Hey, people want balance. If there's a problem, they want a solution. If they have a need, they want that need fulfilled. So if we look at psychology and the human mind, people are looking for answers. There must be a way to organize information that goes along with this natural human thought process . . ."

And Monroe's Motivated Sequence was born. Since then, it's been applied to communication and presentations in almost every possible industry. It helps drive action because when the mind is in a state of unrest, we actively look for a way to bring it back to a state of rest. In other words, when the mind is confused, we need to find a way to remedy the confusion before we can act.

There are five steps in the sequence. You need them all to be maximally effective.

Step One: Attention

Of course you need to get people's attention before you can continue. The goal of this first step is to make sure everyone in the room—physical or virtual—or taking part in the discussion is on the same page. When people are tasked with giving a public speech or presentation in a business setting, we often revert back to basic public-speaking training we may have received, thinking we need to start out with a joke or some other attention-getting tactic.

But in business, clarity tends to be more important. That's not to say you can't use humor and make your presentation fun, but you don't need to overthink it. Sometimes in business this step is built in, and calling a meeting to order is enough. Keeping their attention is the challenge, and we will delve into that in the next step.

Step Two: Establish the Need

The second step in the sequence is to establish the need for your communication (the message, the presentation, why people are gathered, etc.). This is a critical step, and it is not always communicated clearly. Think about establishing expectations and reducing uncertainty. Establishing the need is just that—you need to be crystal clear about why everyone is in the room and needs to listen in the first place. It's also about what you need your audience to contribute to the conversation, and how you want them to behave. This is where you have a chance to unite your audience and put everyone on the same playing field. How you phrase and position the need will vary based on the situation.

FLASHBACK

The importance of reducing uncertainty and establishing expectations is discussed in Chapter 2.

An example of a simple statement establishing the need and the expectations for a problem-solving meeting could be: "We are all here today to solve the problem of our declining sales. Each department brings a different way of approaching sales that is valuable, and your unique perspectives and experiences will help create the solution."

Whereas establishing the need in a sales presentation might look like this: "We're all here to learn about ways to more effectively manage our organization's social media efforts. With the growing number of platforms and channels, keeping up with all of them to make sure customer comments don't fall through the cracks is increasingly difficult. And, unless you're a superhero—and maybe you are—you need a solution to help you manage this so your customers always receive a prompt response."

You're basically getting invisible head nods (or maybe even visible, if you're good) from your audience. They're agreeing with the need. You're all in the same court. Then you're prepared to deliver the one-two punch that is establishing the need and then satisfying it.

As a side note, sometimes you'll see businesses using scare tactics to induce fear when establishing the need. While I'm not going to debate the ethical merits of that here, I will point out that while fear does motivate some people to act, it likely will not create sustained change or continued action. Sketchy businesses use fear as a psychological motivator. Don't be that business! Present the facts and let your audience make up their own minds.

Step Three: Satisfying the Need

Now you have your audience ready for a solution, or ready to contribute to the solution. The third step in the sequence is how you bring that solution to the table. In this step, you typically expand on data or facts that you presented in Step 2 and show how your solution will change the status quo.

If this is a persuasive presentation or a sales pitch, now is the time to unveil your service or product that will solve the problem and satisfy the need. If you're using this structure to organize a team meeting, the satisfaction step is where a lot of the teamwork and individual contributions come into play. This is where people support what they help create. Seek input from team members and have them help craft a solution to the problem.

A word of caution: If you're using the sequence in a presentation where you are the speaker and you have no solution or satisfaction, you're shooting yourself in the foot if you don't allow contributions from the audience in an effort to co-create. It's better to own that you don't have the answer and ask for help than to pontificate about the need without a concrete plan (think about the audience's frustration at presidential—or any political—debates, where problems are raised but no clear solutions are presented).

Step Four: Visualization

You've likely heard the saying, "A picture is worth a thousand words." That statement absolutely applies in the visualization step. Here you help your audience visualize what their world would look like

REAL PEOPLE, REAL STORIES, REAL RESULTS

Peter Shankman

CEO and Founder, ShankMinds: Breakthrough

You Have 2.7 Seconds to Reach Your Audience

Learn to communicate! If you think of a mobile world where we communicate in 140 characters at most, you have to learn to write. You have to learn to speak. And you have to learn to write and speak well. This is non-negotiable.

Having an Audience Is a Privilege, Not a Right

If you have created something or have any content out there that makes people want to listen to you, that's a privilege, and you can lose that tomorrow if you start being full of shit. You have to be incredibly focused, incredibly straightforward, and incredibly honest with your audience. Talk to them. Ask them what they want. Ask them what they like. Ask them how they like to get their information. Give it to them the way they want. Don't deviate from that.

Always Do the Scary Thing

Whatever that scary thing is, do the scary thing. It's so important to do the scary thing. The highway of life is littered with the ghosts of people who never did the scary thing. We don't know the names. We know the names of people who did the scary thing. It's a good business lesson, too.

If You Can Track It, You Can Achieve It

One of the main things I did was I started focusing not on exercise and eating as a thing I had to do but rather as a game of data. Can I track the data? It turns out, if you can track the data in life for anything in the world, that's how you will succeed. The same goes for your business.

Don't Assume What Your Audience Wants Without Asking Them

It just never works. You have to understand your audience. You have to understand what your audience wants. You have to understand where they are. You have to understand how they like to get their information. Understand your audience. Understand how and where they're consuming your content. And use the pathways where your audience is. Do your homework.

Create Non-Deviatable, Self-Actualizing Rules

You create the life you want by putting into effect ways of living that don't really allow you to deviate. We all have the same 24 hours in a day. When people say they "don't have the time," it really means they don't have the desire. They have all the time in the world, but they just have priorities in life that they believe to be more important. Let's call it what it is. You have the time. You just don't have the desire.

if they took the action you're about to request, how their lives would be enhanced if they adopted your solution, the improvements they would see in changing the status quo—in other words, the results they can expect from the solution you're providing. But in Technicolor!

Paint a picture with words. This is where you get to demonstrate the effectiveness of your product or solution by helping your audience picture your solution in their world. This is where it goes beyond information to starting to apply that information in context.

FLASHBACK

If we think back to Chapter 4 on how others listen to us, this stage is a clear way to transition your audience from listening for information to listening for knowledge. And we all know how important that is now!

Step Five: Call to Action

The most overlooked step in business communication is failing to ask for an action. This can mean a meeting where you deliver great information but don't tell your team the next steps. Or where you provide relevant details but fail to tell someone what to do with the information. Or it can simply be failing to ask for the sale.

Sometimes we assume that just because somebody sees the potential, they will act on their own accord. Often, leaders and managers of companies and teams assume that since they're in a position of authority, their employees know how to act—and will eagerly and willingly choose to act—on information that was provided. This assumption can be quite costly.

You don't get what you don't ask for! People can't read your mind.

In this last step, you need to tell people what actions, results, or decisions they need to take or make. In a sales conversation, you're not going to get to the end of your meeting without asking your prospect for their business. The same goes for any meeting, presentation, or speech where you are expecting or hoping for the audience to act. This is also a key place, if you're using the "come full circle" structure, that you can tie back to the first step, where you've gained attention, and bring the presentation to a close.

No matter what organizational structure you use, it's important that any presentation, team meeting, sales conversation, or public speech have some type of organizational pattern. The last thing you want while giving your presentation is your audience wondering where you're going next. A confused mind does not buy. A confused mind does not make decisions. Having clarity about how information is presented, and delivering it in a structure that makes sense to your audience, will drive bigger, better, and faster results.

⊙ ⊙ ⊙

In the next chapter, we'll talk about something that often comes up at the end of, or during, a presentation or meeting—the question-and-answer period. You'll learn about different Q&A situations and strategies for handling these exchanges.

Inner Workings

How to Manage Teams and Meetings and

Get Buy-In

Handle Q&A Like a Boss

Skills for Handling Tough Questions

The question-and-answer period is a chance for your expertise to truly shine. It's in these unscripted, impromptu moments that bits of brilliance often arise. It's an opportunity for speakers to learn how the audience interpreted their presentation, what information they still need to know, and what thoughts remain on their minds. All of this is valuable data to business owners, leaders, managers, and you, as an entrepreneur.

Remember, public speaking and presentations are really just conversations. But many people don't think of them that way—instead, they get through a presentation, get to the Q&A segment, and heave a sigh of relief. This is because they view the Q&A portion as a conversation after the presentation, when they should be considering it part of a broader conversation that they've already begun!

Others are more nervous about the Q&A section than the presentation. This is because you have to be prepared to expect the unexpected. How do you handle questions when you don't know the answer? How do you deal with inappropriate questions? What do you do about questions that cannot be answered within your time frame? And how do you tell the person who's pontificating just to hear himself speak that he needs to cut to the chase and ask a question?

No matter what situation you find yourself in, here are three general strategies for managing Q&A periods. Then we'll look into multiple circumstances in which you might find yourself presented with questions, and present ways of navigating these scenarios so you can best capitalize on all these opportunities.

REAL PEOPLE, REAL STORIES, REAL RESULTS

Andy Crestodina

Co-Founder, Orbit Media

Your Website Has to Answer Questions

I was asked by a client, "If our website just has to do one thing well, what should it do?" My answer was, it has to answer questions. That's really the main function of content. That's the core of all our digital strategies. That's why people visit websites. That's the main use for the internet. Connecting people and answering questions, that's really what it's about.

Read the Minds of Millions to Get Ideas for Content Strategy, Without Guessing

People want to help themselves. They want practical information; they want answers to questions that start with "how to" because they're trying to solve their own problems. It's only after they try that or research a solution themselves that they reach out to a pro. There are simple, free, super-quick research tools that will help you create content that is more empathetic than you might have created otherwise. Answerthepublic.com, FaqFox.com, Google Suggest, and Keyword Tool are some I suggest.

Our Audiences Tell Us the Information They Need, We Just Have to Listen

In B2B, think about what questions people need answered before they will hire you. In B2C, what are the customer service questions? Ask yourself, "Is there an email you send out a lot? Or is there a tweet or a post you have to answer a lot?" If you are answering the same question over and over in your daily communications, you probably should post that answer somewhere on your site. Your sent mail folder and your email outbox are filled with great content. The trick is to unlock it from there and put it on your site and your social streams.

Structure Your Presentations to Answer Questions

When walking into your presentation, people begin with curiosity and gaps in their knowledge. They might not be super articulate about it, but when people come into a session, they want information on that topic. The Q&A format is a super familiar way to structure content. Make the divider slides—the section headers—in your presentation in the format of questions; that gives people a mental paradigm where they know what value you're going to give them.

Every Knowledge Gap Is an Opportunity

We have monthly meetings where we share knowledge. In our team meetings, we'll identify gaps in knowledge. Someone will present an idea that turns into a question, which turns into an opportunity for internal training—a lunch and learn, a sit-down, something virtual. Those are all ways we turn questions the team has into knowledge, which becomes institutionalized by sharing information across teams.

Repeating the Question

One strategy for having time to process questions so you can answer intelligently is to repeat the question back to the person asking. This may sound familiar if you read Chapter 12. Whenever someone asks you a question, you should paraphrase the question back to them. This serves two purposes. The first purpose is to let the rest of the audience hear the question: If the questioner spoke softly, they might not have heard, or if the meeting is being recorded and they didn't use a microphone, you'll get it on record and get everyone in the audience on the same page. The second purpose is to give you time to think and process what your response might be.

This also ensures that you heard and understood the question as the audience member intended it. It's always a good idea to rephrase or paraphrase the original question back to the asker, just to make sure there are no misunderstandings—especially in a presentation situation, where audience members often will not have microphones.

Tie Your Original Material into Responses

The strongest presenters, with the best Q&A sessions, tend to blend their original material with the questions from the audience. This is when true magic can happen. Your presentation likely has about three key points you want to get across. Whenever possible, and whenever it's authentic and natural and organic, tie your original key points back into the answer. This reinforces the information you want to get across, keeps your key points at the top of your audience's mind, and enhances the likelihood of retention.

Managing the Time Suckers

Let's say you have a person who is incessantly asking you questions and taking up a lot of time. You can politely defer them until later by saying, "Thank you, sir. I really appreciate your interest. Let's have a conversation after the presentation one-on-one."

Or say you have someone who is getting up on a soapbox instead of asking a question. It's OK to politely interrupt them and say, "We only have a few minutes for questions. Will you please ask yours?" Or simply ask, "What's your question?"

It's also important to manage the time expectations of others in the room. Any time a person asks a question that is unique to their needs only, it takes valuable time away from the other audience members.

The best way to manage time suckers? Set expectations for the Q&A period right at the outset. Here's one way:

We now have 15 minutes for questions. In order to be fair to all here, please keep your questions brief and to the point. If you have a ques-

*tion that is specific to you and your business, and that's not relevant
to the rest of the attendees, please respect everyone's time and save it
for after the presentation, when I'll be in the hallway to chat.*

These strategies can be used in any meeting situation. Let's look
at some techniques for managing Q&A periods in a few common
business situations: internal meetings, general public meetings, and
consumer meetings.

Internal Meetings

These are meetings where you've gathered your employees, or a group
of employees, for a specific purpose. These could be routine meetings,
such as monthly all-hands meetings, or special meetings that are called
based on a specific need or demand. Sometimes the purpose of an all-
hands meeting is to update on the state of the business or to present
new directions or initiatives. This is where you'll have the opportunity
to discover the questions that linger on your employees' minds. This
is also a great opportunity for you to seek feedback about a certain
program, process, or idea.

In these meetings, it's important that you remind everyone at the
onset of the business's MVVP and tie in what you're doing to serve
that bigger picture.

MVVP stands for mission/vision/values/purpose. Different
companies call them different things, but what is most important
is that the MVVP provides a bigger context for your business and
answers some all-important questions: Why does your company do
what it does, who does it serve, and how, when, and where does it do it?
(You might notice that the WWWWWH—who, what, where, when,
why, and how of Chapter 12 all come into play.)

Here's an example of how you can bring this up seamlessly in a
meeting:

*Today we're going to discuss our new product, and how it helps us
better deliver happiness to our customers. I'm going to give a presentation overviewing the product, recognize the people involved, and
then open it up for questions.*

Notice that the MVVP of the company—delivering happiness to the customer—is presented at the start and tied to the purpose of the meeting. You've given an overview or agenda of the meeting, and you've stated how you're going to handle questions and answers. Bravo.

For each meeting, clearly set the expectations for what type of questions you will be addressing, and how and when you'll be addressing them.

- ⊙ Are you going to address them all at the end?
- ⊙ Will you break for questions throughout?
- ⊙ Do you want people to interrupt the presentation and ask questions as they arise?
- ⊙ Should they send them in on notecards?
- ⊙ Should they type them into Slack or some other internal communication or chat tool?

Is this meeting a time for random grievances to come to the surface? If not, clearly set the stage for acceptable questions, as off-topic issues will detract from the overall purpose of the meeting. Here's one way to do it:

I understand there may be questions about our new health insurance policy. This is not the time to discuss it. We'll have a separate meeting with HR representatives to talk about that situation. Now, we need to focus on this project.

However, sometimes employees just want to be heard. You don't want to discourage this, as that can lead to employees feeling devalued. Instead, use the idea of a parking lot to table or "park" any questions or comments that aren't directly relevant to the topic at hand. This way, the employee can still be heard, but you won't spend valuable meeting time with all your employees or team members getting distracted by addressing non-topical concerns.

SPOILER ALERT

The idea of the parking lot is presented in detail in Chapter 19. When it comes to employees feeling devalued, this can have severe consequences in the workplace. We'll talk about that more in Chapter 22.

Here's another way to handle opening a meeting and setting expectations for questions when you only want a specific type of feedback:

We're all here today to contribute ideas to our new Super Bowl marketing campaign, which focuses on our new support initiatives to better serve our clients. The brand team will give a brief presentation about the campaign development thus far, and then I'll facilitate a Q&A session. The concept is established, so please keep your questions or suggestions related to ideas for spreading this message and campaign further.

Then you'd reiterate the last sentence again at the end of the presentation, immediately before opening it up for questions.

In this example, you called a special meeting, gave an agenda, and then—most relevant to interaction—managed expectations for what types of questions and contributions would be accepted. This way, if anyone went outside those parameters, it would be easy to say, "Please keep your comments and questions focused on how we leverage our reach."

General Public Meetings

The next type of meeting or presentation is with a general audience. This audience consists of members of the general public or people outside your organization. In other words, an external audience. With these meetings, keeping consistency with your brand integrity and image is important. If you're giving a presentation to a general audience, the array of questions that may be presented to you is likely to be vast. In these situations, it helps to have someone on hand to record the questions, so that if you cannot address them in the moment due to time constraints or lack of data, you can get back to them at a later date. Follow-up here is essential.

Often companies will simulcast public meetings to a virtual audience. If you're going to do that and still have a Q&A, it is important to make sure that you're able to get questions from both the virtual and in-person audiences. Sometimes this involves having written questions passed to you, instead of providing an open mic on the presentation room floor.

The same tips for organizing meetings apply in these situations— setting expectations clearly at the beginning and following the general rules presented earlier for managing questions and answers.

Consumer Meetings

Another type of Q&A situation is when you're speaking to a potential consumer or consumer audience. In these instances, it's important to directly address any questions pertaining to your product or service, follow-through, implementation, or utility. Of course other questions are important as well, but those four types will leave you the most vulnerable if they remain unanswered.

In these forums, complaints or frustrations could rise to the surface. If you anticipate that happening, it's always a good idea to have a member of support staff or a technical product expert on hand who can answer those questions so the meeting doesn't get derailed. For instance, if you are not a programmer and you're speaking to an audience about a new software development, it may be useful to have a programmer or a tech-support person in the room to address any concerns from a user perspective.

It's always important to be direct. If you don't know the answer to a question, admit it and request contact information for a personalized follow-up. As I emphasized in Chapter 17, a confused mind does not buy, act, or make decisions. The Q&A session is one valuable point in time for you to alleviate fears, clarify misunderstandings, and entice your audience to act.

⊙ ⊙ ⊙

In the next chapter, we'll talk about strategies that expand on how to run effective and efficient meetings. You'll see some of the expectation-setting strategies presented in this chapter come into play.

All Hands on Deck!

Effective and Efficient Meetings

A lot of people cringe when they see "let's set up a meeting" in an email or instant message. I understand. Many organizations have meetings just for the sake of having meetings, where people feel forced to come up with something to talk about. These meetings, without a clear purpose or goal, are why they get a bad rep. But meetings are an essential part of business. And learning to run them effectively and efficiently can help you be a better manager and leader. Here are some strategies for making your meetings work for you.

Dual-Purpose Meetings

Your meetings should always have a dual purpose—the purpose for the meeting itself and the purpose in the broader organizational context. Let's examine both a bit further.

Make sure your meetings have a clear purpose. This seems obvious, but it needs to go beyond "We need to catch up" or "It's been awhile since we've met." You need to be specific. Even if it's just that you want to get to know an employee better and learn how he's faring in his new role, a simple "Let's chat" isn't enough. Instead, communicate your intent and purpose.

> *Hi, Jim. We haven't had much time to chat since you started working here, and I'd like to talk about how the position is working out for you, and how you see your role within the company.*

That's going to set a clear intention and will help communicate the meeting's purpose for both parties involved.

But when it comes to meetings having a dual purpose, it's not just the purpose of the meeting itself, but also the purpose the meeting has in the overall picture of the organization that's important. Studies show that one key factor in employee retention is that employees need to feel connected to a greater purpose, or a greater "why," in their work. If you tie your MVVP into your meetings, it will remind people of the purpose of their work.

> **FLASHBACK**
>
> MVVP is presented in Chapter 18; it stands for mission/vision/values/purpose.

It may seem superfluous, but you have a key chance to reinforce the MVVP of your business in an easy, natural way. Here's a simple format:

> *We're having a meeting to discuss X, which helps us Y.*

Here, X is the meeting purpose and Y is the organizational purpose.

Know the Rules of Engagement

We all need to know what game we're playing. If I'm coming to a meeting expecting to go by the rules of football but we're playing rugby, we're going to have problems (especially with the differences in equipment and padding, yikes!).

Nobody likes to be unprepared. The last thing I want to do is go into my manager's office without the specific data or report I need, when I thought we were just having a quick check-in on my way back from lunch.

People need to know what the expectations are in any meeting. And you need to establish them prior to the meeting and repeat them at the beginning of the meeting to get everyone on the same page. Before the meeting, make sure your invitation contains these pieces of information:

- ⊙ (Dual) purpose
- ⊙ Goal and/or the desired outcome
- ⊙ Time/date/location (logistics)
- ⊙ What to prepare—this is huge, and a lot of managers assume people will know this. Don't assume!
- ⊙ What to bring—if you want something physically brought to the meeting, be sure you state it explicitly.

Providing an invitation and establishing expectations are also strategies you should use for sales meetings or any communication situation where you need to produce a result or drive action. This ensures that all parties involved get what they need out of the interaction.

Let's say you set up a meeting with a potential client, and you really don't understand what they're hoping to gain from it. How are you going to make sure you meet her needs? Well, you have to ask: "What do you expect me to bring to the table today?" "What do you hope to learn from our meeting today?" "What information would you like me to provide?"

Don't assume. We all know what that can do.

Agendas

Establishing clear expectations by using agendas helps you avoid ambiguity and distraction in meetings. Note that the agenda is different from the invitation, though some of the elements will be present in both.

Here's a simple format for meeting agendas that follows a common organizational pattern in introductions of public speeches and presentations—the three tells.

REAL PEOPLE, REAL STORIES, REAL RESULTS

Michelle Villalobos

Superstar Branding Expert, Mivista Consulting

Audience Size Doesn't Equal Impact

We started out doing big events. The first Women's Success Summit was 600-plus people. But if you're thinking about doing events, look at smaller events very seriously. We have this vision sometimes of doing these humongous things, because we feel like that's the way we can make a bigger impact, when in fact, smaller events are way more profitable, a lot less stressful, and you make a bigger impact . . . on fewer people, but then they go do something bigger and better with it.

Manage Meetings and Communication with Clear Expectations

Managing people and scheduling meetings isn't something that everybody loves. But it's necessary to grow your business. We've designed a schedule where all internal meetings happen on one day of the week. If something comes up in between meetings, of course it gets addressed, but we can rely on those weekly touchpoints. As virtual teams, we keep everything in Google Docs and Dropbox. You have to have great tools for virtual teamwork. We've also found that email is a problem. We have a policy that if something will take more than one email to get resolved, then we pick up the phone and use email as a recap.

Be Accessible in Different Channels, and Meet in Different Formats

In our coaching mastermind groups, what I've found—and experienced—is that a once-a-month, 30-minute meeting doesn't work for everyone. It didn't work for me. I need to have access when I need it. For our mastermind teams, when they need us, we're there. We make a really big effort to be able to support them in the moment when they need it. We also do a weekly call as a group, and we've created a virtual community in WhatsApp.

Create Community, Step Back, and Let Them Take the Wheel

The community creates value that we never could have anticipated, that we never could have created. So take your hands off and let it flourish. What we really manage is the standards and values—that's when we contribute. That's really what makes people have the breakthroughs that they have, is when they start to up-level their standards for themselves, the standards for people they work with, the standards for their clients.

Withholding Information Is a Huge Communication Challenge

In meetings, in teams, in communities, with clients—withholding information is a challenge. When something is difficult, when something is uncomfortable, people tend to avoid it. If people don't speak the unspoken to each other, if you're not willing to tell me your expectations aren't being met, then how can I be of service to you and vice versa? It may be painful, but if you want to grow a business, it has to be part of the culture and it has to happen.

---

1. Tell them what you're going to tell them.
2. Tell them.
3. Tell them what you told them.

In the case of agendas, though, this takes a slightly different form.

What the Meeting Is Going to Do (Tell Them What You're Going to Tell Them)

Give an overview of the purpose and the expectations for the meeting and how to contribute and participate, as well as the goal and desired outcome.

The Bulk of the Meeting and Discussion (Tell Them)

Create your main agenda points. These are the things you need to accomplish, learn, or contribute to the meeting to meet the goal and desired outcome. State the facts and information needed to process the idea or make a decision right at the beginning so there are no lingering unanswered questions.

Summarize the Necessary Actions and Timelines (Tell Them What You Told Them)

This is where so many meetings fall short. Nobody clarifies the next steps! At the end of a meeting, it's imperative to check for mutual understanding, so all parties know the takeaway objectives, directives, and courses of action. This also creates more accountability and responsibility.

This is where you summarize the outcomes of the meeting and clearly state follow-up actions, responsibilities, and timelines that accompany those actions. Have people take responsibility for their individual tasks and state clear deadlines. If you skip this step, your meeting will have been in vain, and you will have wasted a lot of time and energy.

Now that you have strategies for running effective and results-generating meetings, I want to point out two things that can derail or hijack meetings and how to overcome them.

Short- and Long-Term Parking

Many people fail to generate the desired outcome because their meetings lack structure. But after reading the first part of this chapter, you're not going to do that! Still, whenever you get people together in a room (physical or virtual), there's the risk of crosstalk or sidebar conversations or a random question that diverts attention from the original goal. Ignoring these questions completely can result in employees feeling devalued. One strategy to acknowledge the idea but table it for another time is to use an idea parking lot. This is where you put any discussions or topics that arise but aren't pertinent to the task at hand. When you "park" an idea, you're recognizing that the contribution is important but not relevant to the purpose of the meeting.

I like to think of this strategy in terms of both short-term and long-term parking.

Short-Term Parking

This parking lot is for conversations and ideas that need to be addressed to successfully evaluate or complete the team's original charge or goal.

These could be project-related ideas or problems or concerns affecting the successful completion of a project. This parking lot is often a bit more chaotic, as ideas come in and out more frequently and can easily take up unnecessary time in your meetings if you don't curb them quickly. With ideas that are related to the task at hand but not essential to the meeting agenda, it's important to short-term park the conversation to meet the original meeting objectives and then retrieve the idea shortly thereafter.

Long-Term Parking

This parking lot is for conversations and ideas that need to be retrieved after the original goal is met. If an idea comes up that is an important contribution but isn't necessary to complete the team's original charge, put it in long-term parking. Make sure the person whose idea is being parked knows when and where the conversation will be brought back to the surface. This general structure helps you recognize contributions from each team member while still keeping the meeting on track and accomplishing goals.

The Proverbial Elephant

The phrase "the elephant in the room" means that there is something going on external to the present meeting that needs to be dealt with before people can focus on the task at hand. Basically, there's something so big, so important, or so interesting that it will be on people's minds and overrun the meeting unless you address it.

No matter how well you've planned a meeting, if there's a proverbial elephant in the room, meeting productivity will suffer if you don't take time to acknowledge competing concerns.

For example, if there is a major story breaking in the news and people want to be updated, tell the meeting participants that you know there is breaking news, but that you'd appreciate everyone's undivided attention for the next 30 minutes.

It's important to acknowledge any competing concerns that may exist *before* starting a meeting. Do this by using the following three-step process:

1. Acknowledge the elephant
2. Provide a path
3. Regroup and execute

For example, if your company was just acquired by another and everyone is worried about job security, you could say the following.

Step One: Acknowledge the Elephant

I realize that [topic of meeting] isn't at the forefront of our minds today with the recent acquisition. Just like you, I'm worried about what this will mean for my job and all our futures.

Step Two: Provide a Path

Nonetheless, we have a job to do now, and this issue needs our attention. For now, let's focus on [topic of meeting] and designate another time to talk about acquisition concerns.

If you need to do this immediately because of a sensitive issue occupying minds and energy, get the time pinned down for another meeting right then and there. You don't want to just pay lip service to an idea; you want to take action and remove the elephant from the room completely.

Step Three: Regroup and Execute

Now that we have a time and space to talk about the acquisition, let's get back to the task at hand, [topic of meeting], and have a productive meeting.

Then continue on with the meeting agenda you set and distributed prior to the elephant entering the room.

The combination of strategies presented in this chapter will help you run more effective, more efficient meetings that don't make people lament when another meeting appears on their schedule.

⊙ ⊙ ⊙

In the next chapter, we'll expand on what we've learned in this chapter and apply it to a specific type of working team—the virtual team. We'll cover not only meeting strategies, but also tips for better leading these teams through conflict and problem solving.

CHAPTER 20

Cyber Isn't a Dirty Word

Managing Virtual Teams

A team is a group of individuals who share a common goal and are brought together for a unifying purpose. In today's global and distributed business economy, virtual teams are becoming the norm, rather than the exception. Whether you work for, or are contracted with, a large company with a physical office space and are managing a geographically dispersed workforce or you're just getting started with part-time virtual assistants scattered across the globe, learning to manage and communicate with virtual teams is essential to your business growth and success.

In this chapter, we'll go into specific strategies for working with and in virtual teams. In Chapter 19, we talked about organizing effective and efficient meetings. Those strategies and ideas do apply to virtual teams. This chapter will go into more detail on specifically managing the idiosyncratic differences between virtual and physical teams. But first, let's look at some fundamentals that are important to understand for all teamwork—virtual or in person.

Goals vs. Objectives

We already know that a team is a group organized around a specific goal or purpose. But in order to meet a goal—the desired end result—the team must complete many tasks or objectives.

Well-organized teams need to detail both.

At the beginning stages of team formation, state what each person brings to the team and their responsibilities. Stress the importance of interdependence—that in order for the team to succeed, each individual needs to play his or her role. This can also be a time to establish guidelines for team behavior, norms, and any necessary rules.

In leading and managing teams, you want to make sure the roles and purposes for each team member are clear. This is part of being a team leader, delegating responsibility, and holding people accountable. Together you outline the tasks or objectives needed to meet the goal and then divide and conquer (or divide, collaborate in smaller groups, and conquer, if applicable).

Avoid Information Hoarding

One mistake team leaders commonly make is withholding information. This is sometimes done unintentionally and with good will behind it, as you don't want to inundate your team with unnecessary information. But transparency rules if you want the best results.

Don't hoard information! Some people do this out of fear of losing control. But if you want your teams to perform well and be motivated to innovate, don't hold anything back. Good leaders will act as an information hub, where information can flow freely and transparent communication is encouraged.

One way to do this is to create a shared file site (Google Docs, Basecamp, Dropbox, etc.) where any and all relevant information can be stored. Title or categorize the documents clearly so information can be easily accessed. Communicate this to your team, so if they want resources or additional intel, they know where to find it. It's better to put it all there at the outset and give your teams access than to keep it

REAL PEOPLE, REAL STORIES, REAL RESULTS

Brit Morin

CEO and Founder, Brit + Co

Communication Is Probably 90 Percent of My Job

When we were fewer than 20 people, it was really easy for me to keep tabs on everyone and understand what they were doing. I would see them all the time in the office. Now we have more than 100 people, we're in two different offices, we have remote employees and hundreds of contributors. We use Slack internally to foster efficient communication.

Transparency at All Levels Is Key

We do all-hands with the team where I talk about the state of the business and what's going on at every board meeting. I'm really transparent about our board meetings; I go through the entire board deck with the team and talk about the feedback from the meeting.

Weekly Emails to Keep in Touch

Comprised of highlights from the week; shout-outs to people I think are doing a great job or have done something interesting or clever or new; and what I'm thinking about, what I'm excited about, and what I did that week, these emails are a way for employees to keep in touch with what's going on in my head.

Consistent Focus on the Brand Message

We work with a ton of partners and focus on messaging that complements their brand and ours together. I, personally, am constantly talking about Brit + Co. in a public forum as well. And we work on empowering employees and giving them a voice to communicate about the brand and fostering community.

Social Media Adds a Spotlight

A lot of businesses don't want their people on social media, but the thing is they're doing it anyway. Whereas I'm like, "What's the coolest thing you've seen on Snapchat lately? Should we try it? Should we do it?" We have to continue to be authentic about what we're doing and how we treat our employees internally. With social media, the experiences they have at work can be vocalized on all their channels everywhere they go. All my employees, for example, are their own PR outlets.

Bring Down the Wall Between Internal and External Communication

It's not a dichotomy. When you think of the spectrum of communication, when you're balancing these internal and external dynamics here, to me it's about talking to companies about bringing down that wall. It's actually in one huge area, and unless you recognize that information is going to permeate your walls one way or the other, you're not going to ever be able to craft a communication strategy that is authentic and consistent.

to yourself and end up with a less-than-optimal solution because not all available information was used.

Managing Team Conflict

Whenever you have more than one person involved in any activity, conflict is a natural part of business. That's why conflict is often viewed as neutral. It's only negative if you let it get to that point. Without conflict, the status quo prevails. A significant amount of positive change can result from conflict if it's managed correctly.

To understand conflict in your teams better, here are a few of the commonly used conflict management strategies. These strategies are often used to avoid or postpone conflict, but the underlying issue will likely resurface if you don't address the conflict at the root. If you find yourself or a team member using one of these strategies, it's best to address the elephant in the room (remember Chapter 19) and state that while we're going to postpone the conflict for now in the interest of moving the team toward an objective or goal, it needs to be addressed eventually.

Ignoring

Here the conflict is ignored altogether. People walk away, switch topics, or simply ignore the reality. One or both parties will feel inequity at this point, and negative feelings will likely build under the surface. If you see conflict being ignored, as mentioned earlier, note that it is happening and that you will come together and address it at the appropriate time.

Acquiescing

This is when one party just gives up, submits, surrenders, or agrees to disagree to accommodate the other person and end the conflict. Again, the conflict will not truly be resolved unless the root issues are addressed.

Compromising

A compromise is when you give up part of what you want, the other party gives up on something he wants, and you both move forward. A common misperception about managing conflict is to think that compromise is the go-to solution. But compromise isn't a win/win. At best it's a half-win/half-win. Creating win-win solutions involves creative problem solving, a deep understanding of the conflict from both sides, and a willingness to work together toward a solution. This can only come from dialogue, and from really understanding the different personalities, perspectives, and thought processes involved.

Now that you have some fundamentals on managing teams down pat, it's time to focus on specific strategies for communicating and leading virtual teams.

Let's Get Virtual

Research shows that virtual teams can actually be more effective in solving quick, simple problems than in-person teams. However, the more complex the problem, the more there is a need for face-to-face interaction. You know what? There is a theory for that! Allow me a moment to put on my proverbial professor hat and explain.

Picking the right channel, or medium, to communicate your message is important. In the 1960s, an English professor named Marshall McLuhan coined the phrase "the medium is the message." This basically means that the way in which you choose to communicate sends a message in and of itself. If you choose to email instead of stopping by someone's office, for example, that communicates. If you choose to text instead of call, that communicates. McLuhan is right.

A little more than 20 years later, two other dudes—Richard Daft and Robert Lengel—came on the scene and started expanding the conversation about choosing the right media for each message. They examined all different types of media and communication channels and came up with Media Richness Theory. This theory basically says that the richer a medium is, the more visual and auditory cues it is able to convey. Basically, the richer mediums allow communicators to pick up on both verbal and nonverbal messages. Face-to-face communication, then, is the richest medium. Text, on the other hand, is the least rich. The key is to match your media choice to the message you have to send. The more complex the message, the richer the medium you need. Here's a graphic to help illustrate (Figure 20–1 on page 189).

With virtual teams, you don't have the option of meeting face-to-face. But you can get as close to that as possible. Advancements in technology have made it considerably easier to coordinate virtual, visual meetings with people across the globe. Videoconferencing is no longer limited to organizations with deep pockets. Your phone is now a videoconferencing device. Applications like Skype, Google Hangouts, and—my favorite—Zoom have enabled and facilitated this visual communication. The important thing is to choose the medium that best fits the task you're trying to accomplish, not the one that is the most convenient.

Virtual Kickoffs

Prior to starting work with any virtual team, have your first meeting via videoconference. This allows each person on the team to "put a face

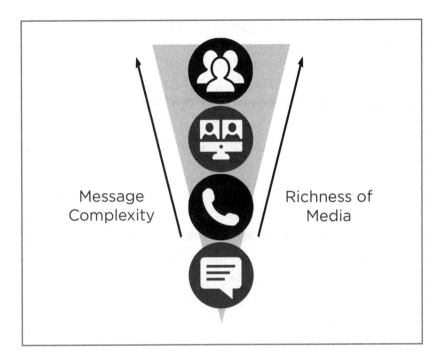

FIGURE 20-1

Media Selection Tool

to a name" and establish a visual rapport with each team member. If you're a consultant coming in from outside, this is even more essential, as you don't have an established culture with the group already. Set this standard early. You can do this as a kickoff meeting to introduce everyone involved, establish responsibilities, and celebrate the mutual goal that the team will work toward achieving together.

At the outset, agree on the technologies you'll use for communication. What are the channels you agree to monitor? What hours will you make yourself available? Set these expectations right off the bat and stick to the plan. Is email the best choice? Is there a better tool for your project (Slack is increasingly popular)? What's the expected turnaround time? What's the policy on replying to all vs. replying to only the relevant parties? When should someone just pick up the phone (or get on a video call) and talk instead of having an email chain go back and forth?

Establishing communication norms and rules at the beginning will save time and frustration later in the process.

If you're managing your whole business as a virtual team, have periodic all-hands or town-hall meetings via video and record them so those who were unable to attend may still glean any necessary information. Summarize your virtual meetings in an email to ensure everyone is on the same page, responsibilities are listed, and you can hold everyone accountable.

⊙ ⊙ ⊙

In the next chapter, we'll talk about a strategy you'll use in almost every business communication situation—communicating for buy-in. It goes beyond just persuasion and focuses on how you can really rally the people in your organization around a cause.

Get People on Your Side

Communicating for Buy-In

You've likely heard the phrase "people support what they help create" more than once. There's a reason for that—it's true! No business succeeds in isolation. There's a whole team and community of people—your employees, investors, clients, shareholders, board, partners, vendors, and beyond—that help your business grow. In the introduction to this book, we talked about the importance of recognizing your three simultaneous audiences. When you think about getting buy-in, keeping these three audiences in mind is essential.

Buy-in is not quid pro quo. It's not an "if you do this I'll support you in that" situation. If you're communicating to an audience whose buy-in you need to succeed, you need to think strategically about your messaging, your communicative efforts, and how they're being inclusive of the people you need, and want, to be involved. People like to feel like they belong to something bigger than themselves. Find a way to get people on board with your vision and plan, and with the co-creation process, and you'll find quicker success.

Building a solid value base, getting buy-in from your employees, and cultivating a community of advocates around your products and services are what sustain businesses over time. While they may manifest in flashy merchandising techniques or the latest snap-pin-book-twit-agrams, it's not the manifestation that matters—it's the core message behind the company and the people who support it that have staying power.

Even when you think you have it all figured out, giving your communities an opportunity to contribute is important, and you may be surprised at the ideas that come forward, the responsibility that others are willing to step up and take, and the overall better end result.

In fact, businesses have been based off of creating spaces for people to buy into ideas that they like and believe in. Think of Kickstarter, GoFundMe, and similar crowdfunding sites that built businesses because people want to be part of something bigger than themselves. Think of open source software programs with incredibly loyal developers and crowdsourcing websites where everyone benefits from collective knowledge contributions (Wikipedia). The need to foster buy-in to be innovative, bring awareness to issues, and harness the forces of collaboration is clear.

What happens if you don't create buy-in? Feelings of isolation, declining employee and consumer retention, and negative brand impacts are just a few consequences.

The Magic of Collaboration

Getting buy-in from your internal audience—your employees—keeps your teams feeling like they are an integral part of the company's overall MVVP. It also leads to employees willingly taking on more responsibility and demonstrating higher accountability. Plus, it's good to know your team has your back. Internal buy-in cultivates a feeling of team achievement and victory when an endeavor is successful. Be sure to create and share the celebrations, too. This only reinforces an employee's connection to the project and the business.

Externally, you want to foster a community of users, clients, consumers, and advocates who are motivated to proactively communicate with you when problems arise. When you have customers who will come to you with concerns, ideas, or other feedback, you know they are invested in the success of your business. Empowering your consumers to share ideas for product improvement, your website and marketing, your interaction with them, etc., can lead to feelings of inclusion and that you're more than a vendor—you're a partner. This happens when businesses actively respond to all consumer and external communication. As we discussed in Chapter 6, providing this 24/7 access and response is essential.

When you communicate to an audience to get their buy-in, you want to make sure you're getting their perspective, thoughts, and feelings and taking them into consideration when crafting and presenting your message. By doing so, you will let the audience know you've taken the time to understand them. They will then feel more invested in what you have to say because they will better understand how it relates to them and the task at hand. When you communicate for buy-in, you make people engage. You want to engage people in a way that empowers them to act on whatever message you're delivering. The magic is in the collaboration and the compounded impact it provides.

Unknowingly, though, some people communicate in a way that is counter to buy-in. Let's take a look at a few things that can derail the buy-in process.

> **FLASHBACK**
>
> Remember the concept of Panopticon-style service from Chapter 6? This definitely can help you foster an engaged consumer community that buys in to your vision. It can also help you develop brand ambassadors, which are discussed in the "Real People. Real Stories. Real Results" section of Chapter 16.

Creating Unnecessary Distance

We discussed this in an earlier chapter on delivery and persuasion in terms of nonverbal barriers, and those concepts hold true here as well. If collaboration is your goal, speaking from a podium and keeping people at a distance isn't the best way to communicate that you genuinely want their input. Of course, in large audiences this may be unavoidable, but if you have the choice, sit down at the table with your teams. Get on a level playing field. The power distance you put between yourself and an employee or consumer when you're standing and speaking *over* them, instead of *to* them, creates a counterproductive hierarchy.

When people feel they are "lower," it leads them to believe their ideas won't be considered as strongly. That's the last thing you want to do! Similarly, meeting in a formal office space with a large desk between you and another person, or with your chair raised intentionally higher (seriously, people are insecure enough to make this nonverbal power play), will stop the free flow of conversation. Don't put unnecessary barriers between you and your audience, whether an audience of one or thousands.

REAL PEOPLE, REAL STORIES, REAL RESULTS

Greg Rollett

CEO and Founder, Ambitious.com

It All Comes Down to Storytelling

The root of everything, to me, comes down to storytelling. The best marketers are the best storytellers. When it comes down to it, a brand is nothing more than a story, and the best brands in the world are the best storytellers. Stories get people interested, engaged, and emotionally connected. For solo entrepreneurs and personality driven entrepreneurs, we have to go out and we have to tell our story. The more ways that we can tell our story and the more places that we can tell our story, the better.

Sharing Your Faults and Failures Attracts People

I think the hardest thing for people to get across is sharing some of their faults, their failures, their war wounds, if you will, because they're insecure about it. They're scared that if they tell someone that it might detract business, but we found exactly the

---

opposite. The more you go out there and you talk about some of those lessons, some of those failures, some of those pain points, some of the tough times that you've gone through in your life, the more people are attracted to you. I tell those stories. It's those flaws that connect us and bond us more as people than the wins.

Don't Assume That Someone Knows Your Story

Whether you're a solo entrepreneur or a manager, a big mistake people make is they assume their audience knows their story. This is a big no-no. Whether it's your personal story or the company story, it needs to be told. Although you may have told that story millions of times to audiences everywhere, you have to retell it, because if someone just comes in, they have no frame of reference for who you are, what you do, and why you do it. It's why at the beginning of every Batman movie, they show his parents getting killed and him turning into Batman. Otherwise, Batman's just a crazy guy in a cape running around Gotham City terrorizing people.

Give Employees a Purpose to Achieve Buy-In

Every day my team comes in. And nearly every day I'm telling a story that illustrates a point. I'm telling a story of how a client used something that we did. I'm telling the stories of people we work with who come into the studio and produce classes with us. I think more so than just story, it's giving your team some purpose for what they're doing, giving them the mission, the higher-level type thing, because it's easy as a leader to just assign tasks. Everybody wants more than just a paycheck. You're going to spend a large portion of your life at the office, at work, doing emails, team meetings, etc. By giving them more of a purpose, it's going to make them more engaged in the work and make them want to do the work.

Inclusive and Exclusive Talk

Sometimes there are unintentional ways you may be demoralizing, demotivating, and quite frankly pissing your audiences off. Inclusive and exclusive talk is one of those ways. What on earth am I talking about? Glad you asked.

Inclusive and exclusive messaging strategies can help put people into the "in" group or make them feel ostracized in the "out" group.

So if you don't want to alienate people from your cause or your relationships, you want to be inclusive in your messaging. But how do you do that? Inclusive messages draw others in and make others feel like a part of a project, a part of the plan. With inclusive messages, you're inviting people to be a part of the group. You're inviting them to belong.

Unintentionally, managers often refer to hierarchical groupings—us and them. This polarizes your audiences. If you talk about the "management team," anyone who is not a part of that team is now in the "out" group. Being aware of how this affects potential buy-in and people's willingness to come forward with contributions and ideas is important.

Let's say you have a new team member who brings new ideas to the table, but they're a little different from anything your business has ever done. If you say something like, "We don't do things like that here," or, "That's not our process," the employee is now excluded from feeling like part of the team. She is now in the "out" group. Additionally, these are polarizing comments—"we" don't do this, and you aren't part of that "we" yet. Her contribution or idea was shot down, and she'll be less likely to proactively share ideas in the future.

Confirming and Disconfirming Messages

Each and every one of us has our own self-concept—what we think we are, where we think we fit, how we think we are valued, who we think supports us, when we're at our best. Messages you receive that are consistent with your self-concept are *confirming* messages—they confirm your identity. The opposite, then, would be *disconfirming* messages, as they present a contrast, opposition, or rejection to our identities.

A disconfirming message might be, "I thought you'd know more about this," or "I wish you would've done more," or "This isn't the quality I expected from you." These messages in isolation can cause problems with morale, feelings of inequity, or worse. But sometimes you need to point out something so it can be corrected.

If you're going to send a disconfirming message, it's important to follow it with a conversation that provides courses of action for the person to take that will right the wrong. You don't want to tell someone "I really don't like what you did with this project" without giving them a course of action to correct it, because without that course of action you're just criticizing them without any constructive feedback. That disconfirms their identity, which will make them—as a partner, as an employee, as a friend—not want to build a continual relationship with you. Kiss their buy-in goodbye.

SPOILER ALERT

We'll talk about feedback and how to give it in a way that delivers results in Chapter 23. You can deliver a disconfirming message effectively when you make it specific and follow it with actionable course correction messaging.

⊙ ⊙ ⊙

In the next chapter, we'll talk about the concept of equity in the workplace. This is important, as most personnel issues that have to do with non-skill-based behavior stem from something to do with fairness—or perceived fairness.

PART

VII

Like a Boss

Leading and Managing So People Want to Work

For and With You

22

Fairness Equals Profit

Tenets of Workplace Equity

’ve never heard anyone say, "Please, treat me unfairly." As humans, we want to be treated equitably. We want to know that we are valued, that our work matters, and that we are compensated fairly for our efforts.

While this chapter focuses on employee equity, wanting to be treated fairly is not just relevant to your employees. Your clients crave equity, too. If they don't feel they're getting an equitable exchange of value for their investment, they're not likely to be repeat customers. The concept of equity is about looking at a situation and identifying the variables—the people involved, the resources at play, and the situational factors—and then ask yourself (and answer objectively):

- ⊙ Are we giving each person the necessary resources?
- ⊙ Are we giving each person a proportional amount of attention?
- ⊙ Are we showing appreciation in a balanced way?
- ⊙ Are we giving each person an equal opportunity to succeed?

If you want to be a respected boss, a revered manager, and a followed leader, you need to understand the four tenets of workplace equity.

Let's take it back to the playground. You're in elementary school. It's recess time. You just got a brand-new ball that you brought to school. And you're playing foursquare with some friends. You're passing the ball back and forth, bouncing it from square to square, and then all of a sudden one of your so-called friends grabs the ball and ends the game, walking away with your new toy.

How do you feel?

You're probably pissed. So what are you going to do? Maybe you go up to your friend and grab the ball back, and decide never to share with her again. Maybe you go tell the playground monitor and get your ball back that way (but some would call you a tattletale). Maybe you decide to let your friend keep the ball but vow never to talk to her again. Or maybe you pitch a fit and start crying.

Hey, you're a kid—you might be able to get away with that.

But you won't be able to get away with it in the workplace.

In fact, if you go running to your boss every time something just doesn't go your way, you're going to look far worse than the person who offended you in the first place.

As a manager, you've likely had an employee come to you like this proverbial crying child. While it may be annoying, there's a reason it's happening. Once you understand the four tenets of equity, you'll know better how to communicate dynamically to get to the root of the problem, manage the situation, and ensure a fair solution.

Tenet One: People Exchange Work for Rewards

People work for rewards. Plain and simple. I don't know anybody who goes to a job and doesn't expect to get anything in return. Many managers assume that the salary, hourly wage, or contract rate for coming to work is enough. But they are wrong. In fact, the number-one reason people quit their job is bad bosses, not bad wages.

Your employees, contractors, vendors, and all workplace relationships (really, all relationships in your life) need to feel they're being compensated fairly for the value they're providing. In a managerial capacity, you need to know what makes your employees tick. This compensation is not just monetary. Increased responsibility, availability of resources, collaborative opportunities, continual feedback, managerial support, and professional-development opportunities are all ways to reward employees. At the end of the day, employees want to know they are getting just as much as they are putting in, and that they're making a difference in the workplace and beyond.

If you want to treat employees equitably, don't assume all rewards are created equal for all employees. For example, a $100 restaurant gift card is not going to make Dylan feel the same way as Jaime. Dylan would much rather have a card to a bookstore. Blanket and generic signs of appreciation often fall flat because they assume everyone is the same and show that you're treating everyone the same. The best managers know how each employee likes to be rewarded. In the same vein, your customers like to be rewarded and shown gratitude and appreciation in unique ways.

If you want to retain customers, it's important to treat them as individuals and understand their unique needs and considerations. If you want to show appreciation to your clients, don't just send out one generic gift or "thank you." Make it something unique to each individual client. That is a reward that matters.

Don't send everyone the same box of gourmet chocolates. While it may be a nice gesture, it can also backfire. This happened to a friend with her business. Names are changed to protect the innocent.

"Hi, Robert, I wanted to make sure you received the gift I sent, and let you know how much I appreciate your business."

"I did receive them. It was a nice gesture, but I'm allergic to chocolate. My staff enjoyed them, though."

Oops. That didn't go over as well as intended. Treat people as individuals. Get to know what type of rewards matter. You'll see the difference it makes.

Tenet Two: People Actively Search for Empowering Environments

In addition to working for rewards, we also seek to work in environments where we are treated fairly, and where we are empowered to contribute in a

> **SPOILER ALERT**
>
> In Chapters 26 and 27 we talk about strategies for uniquely recognizing employees and fostering innovation.

meaningful way. If the first tenet is met, employees feel more pride and responsibility in the work they perform. To take this further, empower your employees and provide them with the resources necessary to grow. When employees feel a company is invested in their success, they're more likely to work harder and produce more.

A lack of professional-development opportunities is one of the top reasons people leave jobs. When you're onboarding new employees or recruiting top talent, this type of environment is what will attract.

To foster this environment, leaders need to know what makes each person motivated, what professional aspirations employees have, and how to best empower each and every person. Gaining this information requires dynamic, proactive communication.

Among the Millennial—and upcoming Gen Z—population, catering to the innovative and entrepreneurial spirit is a key retention strategy. According to the Kauffman Foundation, 54 percent of Millennials have a desire to start their own business, with estimates of this number growing up to 72 percent in the post-Millennial, Gen Z population. Cater to this entrepreneurial spirit by empowering employees to innovate. Set up programs for intrapreneurship that allow employees to create within your organization. Make sure your top performers have the resources they need, and the support from their managers, to continue to develop.

Tenet Three: People Feel Stressed When They're Treated Unfairly

Inequity breeds disappointment. Disappointment yields stress. Stress results in a loss of productivity. When employees feel they are being treated unfairly, they become less productive.

REAL PEOPLE, REAL STORIES, REAL RESULTS

Jared Kleinert

Author, *3 Billion Under 30*

The Traditional Path Is Not the Only Path Anymore

We've seen the alliances between employees and employers and the relationship between employees and employers drastically change. Smart companies will go into an arrangement looking for the best alliance between what an employee needs, what expertise they have, and what they want to learn and gain from an experience.

The Relationship Between Employer and Employee Is Changing

You can be an employee in a lot of ways: a traditional employee; a startup founder who's in an incubator run by a corporation that has a stake in your business; a 1099 contractor for multiple businesses. You can move to another company. The relationship doesn't begin and end with a contract. Post-contract, you can still provide a company value by giving referrals for new hires or sending business because they treated you right.

Every Employee Is Different—Quit Putting Them in the Same Basket

Don't assume that all Millennial employees are the same. Instead of grouping employees together, ask one-on-one what a person wants, needs, and desires in an alliance, and then try to offer that in return. I think everyone should be asking that of a potential hire. Then you can learn what that individual wants in terms of learning and training, or potential mobility within an organization.

This Also Applies to Contractors and Freelancers

The same discovery of wants and needs that you do for your employees should also be done for every type of business partnership. Finding good partnerships takes time and effort. Contractors know that and have leverage in terms of bringing their talent to the table or not. Then it goes back to what is that person getting in return? Is it simply finances, or is it the ability to grow a personal brand, work on an interesting project, and/or gain more case study material?

Collaboration and Follow-Through

If you're going to collaborate with people and get their input, be sure you're doing something with that information. Whether you heard ideas and accepted them, or heard them and then rejected them for various reasons, explain those reasons. If you hear advice and use it, follow up with people and let them know you used it. That is going to close the feedback loop and further engage your team.

If an employee finds out a peer is making more money for performing the same role, a manager is spending extra time with one person, or someone's ideas are unfairly favored, productivity suffers. The employee's attention is focused on the stress-inducing act instead of the task at hand.

Note: Perception is reality. When people feel they are being treated unfairly, they will work to redress the perceived inequity.

How do you know whether employees feel they are being treated unfairly? The obvious answer is to simply ask them. But when you do, be prepared to act on the response.

Nobody enjoys feeling like their ideas have no merit. A common mistake managers make is asking employees for their thoughts, opinions, and ideas, but not following through with communication or implementation (why these thoughts, opinions, and ideas were or were not acted upon). If you're going to ask a question, be prepared to respond with words and actions. If it is a feasible request, work to make it happen. If it's not actionable now but may be in the future, communicate why and work with the employee on an interim solution. If it's not realistic at all, explain why and ask what other ideas the employee has to continue the discussion.

Take this exchange, for example:

Manager: "What's one thing you'd like to change about your current job responsibilities?"

Employee: "I really enjoy what I do, but I'd like the chance to learn other areas of operations within the company."

Manager: "OK. Great."

Then the conversation ends. The manager takes notes, but never acts. The employee feels undervalued and looks to restore equity. We're now entering the danger zone, and not in a *Top Gun* kind of way.

Instead, of a simple "OK. Great." with no actionable follow-up or plan, say something that recognizes the idea and follows-up with a plan.

> *"I think that's a wonderful idea. Why don't you work out a plan that allows 20 percent of your week for this. I'll review it with you in two weeks and we'll go from there."*

Or, if you aren't able to accommodate the request immediately:

> *"Thanks for sharing that with me. I think it's a great idea. Because of our current structure and staffing we can't afford to do it this quarter. The team needs 100 percent of your expertise and focus on your current role. However, next quarter we can get this started."*

Either way recognizes that the idea was received, and provides a plan for next steps. If you don't do this, people are likely going to seek balance, and the impacts on your business will be more damaging.

Tenet Four: People Who Feel Like They're Treated Unfairly Will Seek to Balance the Scales

Let's look at a scenario. You've been in your current position for a year. It's your first annual review. You've met and well exceeded your $1 million sales goal and are excited to receive your bonus. You get your check and are feeling pretty good about the situation. Until you find out that another employee who has been with the company for five years and met (but did not exceed) the same goal is receiving nearly double your bonus compensation.

This scenario happens. Sometimes bonuses are calculated not just on certain goals, but also on company tenure. But if you're the newer employee who exceeded your sales goal, you probably are screaming in your head, "Huh?! But I sold *more* than this person! How is this fair?!"

Even though the bonus structure may have been laid out in a contract, this will still be a smack in the face to the high-performing employee. Since we know perception is reality, and that this employee's perception is now one of feeling undervalued and unfair, what's likely to happen?

The new person now feels a huge sense of inequity. Some of the thoughts going through this employee's mind could be:

- ⊙ *"Why am I not getting more money? That doesn't seem right."*
- ⊙ *"Why am I not getting as much as him? We met the same number."*
- ⊙ *"What am I not doing right? Am I not doing as well in something else?"*
- ⊙ *"Why am I not appreciated? Is this the right place for me?"*
- ⊙ *"Do I need to go find another job? Clearly they don't value me here."*

If you anticipate feelings of inequity, it's best to address them proactively. This way even though an employee may feel a bit of a blow, he will have heard it directly from, and will have had a chance to communicate about it with, you.

If unaddressed, these thoughts can lead to actions and behaviors that aren't productive or profitable—in fact, just the opposite. It may be reducing the amount of work done. It may be slowing the work pace and spending time messing around with your co-workers, which will then decrease their productivity. It may be causing disruption. It may be expressing your frustration and feelings of inequity with other employees. None of these are positive outcomes for your business.

If you feel you're being treated unfairly, you're likely to do something about it. The same goes for your employees. As a leader, make sure to address inequities—and perceived inequities—before they get to this last stage. Your bottom line will thank you. And so, which is even more important, will your employees.

⊙ ⊙ ⊙

In the next chapter, we'll discuss one of the most important types of communication in the workplace—feedback. You'll use the techniques presented to drive change in your business and learn how to have conversations that create behavioral change in your employees.

Feed Me, Seymour!

Delivering Powerful Feedback That Gets Results

Feedback is the communication oil that keeps the organizational engine running smoothly.

The problem is that so many businesses look at feedback as one-way, or—even worse—they put it in a once-a-year formal performance review. Feedback should be a two-way street. There should be dialogue, there should be exchange, there should be movement in both directions. If there's not, you're not delivering feedback, you're giving orders!

And, for the love of pizza, please don't just have a feedback conversation when there's something that needs to be corrected. Do them routinely, and share the positives as well as the to-be-corrected-and-turned-into positives (otherwise known as negatives, but that's not so fun).

Studies across the board show that giving more frequent feedback results in a more productive, motivated, and engaged workforce. Having frequent performance or feedback conversations is a great way to allow the employee to help build her position in your business. It also reduces feelings of uncertainty or ambiguity because people will always know where they stand, where they fit, and how they contribute.

If you're enabling your employees to help create this feedback conversation, they're more likely to be invested. When you have proactive conversations, the employee is more likely to actually tell you what he needs and will bring some great ideas to the table in the process.

Here are some rules (more like a checklist) you can use to evaluate your feedback messages and make them stronger and more likely to result in action—in other words, let's make them dynamic!

REAL PEOPLE, REAL STORIES, REAL RESULTS

Dan Schawbel

NYT Bestselling Author and Founder, WorkplaceTrends

Create More In-Person Experiences for Employees

The number-one trait people look for in leaders is communication. Communication is king, and regardless of your age, whether you're 16 or 65, unanimously people prefer in-person communication over using technology. As a culture we're almost moving more and more away from actually physically being around other people, but our need to be around other people is accelerating.

Not Communicating Often Enough Comes with a Cost

When you don't communicate often enough, the people you're surrounded by, whether they're employees or friends, don't know where they stand. They might not know what priorities are. They might not know when you actually need something delivered. You have to close all those gaps or risk disengagement. Regular meetings, regular calls, regular feedback, regular check-ins—they are all necessary for an engaged workforce.

Communicate About Doing Social Good

A lot of companies do a lot of social good, but they do a horrible job of communicating the good work they do, internally and externally. People—employees, candidates, and

---

customers—want to know the "why" of a business, and they shouldn't have to ask. Communicate what you're doing to serve the local community, the charities you're involved with, or—better yet—create volunteer programs to let your people feel like part of a solution.

It's All About the Candidate and Employee Experience

If you don't give employees a good experience, they'll look elsewhere. If you don't give candidates a good experience, they'll never apply at your company again. Social media and technology amplify these voices. Ignoring this could really hurt your revenue. Open communication about what the business is doing or where an application is in the review process are relatively simple things that make a big difference.

The Hidden Job Market Is Driven by Relationships

In a world where there's so much clutter, there's so much competition. The people who end up still succeeding are the ones who focus on building a good community and becoming a valuable resource to that community. Relationships are like a fail-safe—a recovery mechanism—as in if you build a large network you almost never have to worry about getting a job or getting new business because it's there for you. I think you're always in a good position if you do that, and the best jobs are the ones you can't even apply for.

Break Down Communication Barriers

People have more choices than ever before. Companies that want to retain employees need to create a great corporate culture. People want meaningful work, but they also want to know what's going on in the company and to be involved in the decision-making process. Open up the doors to your boardroom. Lower boundaries. Have more open conversations. Be more transparent.

Own Your Message

Many make the mistake of starting a feedback conversation with the word "you." Don't do that! Starting out a conversation with the word "you" is the equivalent of verbal finger pointing. It puts someone immediately on the defensive. Pointing fingers and saying "you" is not an opening for a conversation, it's not an opening for discussion, and it's not feedback. You're actually making a declarative statement toward them.

Instead, start your feedback conversation with the word "I" and own your message. "I want to talk about . . ." "I need to see . . ." "I notice . . ." The word "you" can still be in the sentence, but owning the statement from the beginning is important and takes a strong stance.

Another mistake along the lines of not owning your message is the "It might just be me, but . . ." comment. This is not a powerful statement. This weakens your position and any directives that follow.

Owning your message distinguishes you from the people who are afraid to own their feelings, their responsibilities, and their actions. Don't let that be you. Own your message. If you want to be a strong, confident, and powerful leader, manager, and rock-star boss, owning your message is the place to start.

Stop Apologizing and Generalizing

I've worked with too many managers who start off a feedback conversation like this: "I'm sorry we need to have this conversation today, but . . ."

Now, is that an inaccurate statement? No, not necessarily, but you're already saying you don't want to be part of the conversation, which can communicate disinterest. That can send a mixed message to the employee. Don't do that!

Don't apologize for your feelings. Don't apologize for your observations. Don't apologize for your or the organization's needs. Not if you want to drive action. If you want results from your feedback conversations, don't downplay the corrective effect.

Generic feedback, the "We all" or "I've been told" statements, is not effective. Remember Chapter 21, when we talked about "in" and "out" groups? Well, this is one way to immediately put someone on the outside. Hearsay conversations are not generally well-received. Many will actually ask, "Who is 'we'?" or "Who has told you?" And unless you're prepared to throw those people under the bus, you'd better not make generalized comments.

Be Specific and Behavior-Focused

When having feedback conversations, focus on behaviors, not characteristics. A mistake I see many make is mislabeling or misattributing a behavior for character. There is an important distinction here.

A behavior is an act. The same behavior repeated multiple times can become character. Just because someone is late once or twice doesn't make them a tardy person. Their behavior was one of tardiness in a couple of situations. There is a big difference. Just as if you and your family do a certain celebration for a holiday one year, that doesn't make it a tradition. Traditions come after repeated performances. Repeated behavior is character. One or two events in isolation is not.

Someone might make an arrogant statement, but calling that person arrogant communicates something entirely different. Make sure that instead of characteristics you are focusing on behaviors. This is very important and again helps you avoid labeling employees and putting them on the defensive.

It's really important to have the specifics because you need data to back up your statements, or at least very detailed examples, qualitative or quantitative. Then you need to be focused on the behavior, the action that someone did. Focus on results and capabilities—that's the kind of feedback that is generally productive and really necessary.

Another way to be specific is to explain the cause and effect—the behavior and the consequence. "Because of X behavior, Y result was not able to be accomplished."

Facilitate the Desired Outcome with Verbal and Nonverbal Harmony

Actions speak louder than words. We've already talked about the importance of this for delivering a public speech or presentation, but the same is true for feedback conversations. If you want feedback that produces results, your actions and your words must be synonymous; your nonverbal and verbal communication must match.

You don't want to be grinning when you're delivering a serious message (let's be honest; that's just creepy). You don't want to come across as angry even though you may be legitimately frustrated. Believe me, I get it, but if you go into a feedback conversation and come across as angry, you are going to really reduce, if not eliminate, the possibility for a true conversation to occur, as you'll immediately put the employee on the defensive or have them change only as the result of fear. Fear-based changes are not sustainable.

For example, if you catch an employee in a lie, there is a reason they lied. Finding out that reason is going to be way more beneficial to you and your business than yelling at them, no matter how much you may want to. If you yell, you'll never get down to the truth. Behind every lie is a truth (or a perception) that needs to be handled. Get to that, and you'll be back on the right page.

Simple Examples of Great Feedback

Let's look at an example of all these guidelines in practice: talking to an employee who is showing up late.

> *I noticed you have been late three out of the last four Mondays, Brady. That's not your typical pattern. Has something changed in your life that is causing this, or do we need to make an adjustment?*

You owned your message ("I noticed"). You didn't apologize. You were very specific (late three out of four Mondays). And you didn't attack his character and focused only on the behavior and attempted to get to the cause ("has something changed").

This will open up a conversation. And now, perhaps, you can get to the root of the problem together and figure out how to address it.

(It turns out that Brady's partner just took a new job and together they're figuring out how to best share their one car and each get to work on time. A simple schedule adjustment, and no more tardiness. Aren't you glad you got to know something about your employee and were able to create a solution together?)

Let's take another quick example. One of your sales representatives isn't meeting his numbers. You need him to hit those numbers, but you know simply saying, "Hey, Marcus, you need to hit those numbers" isn't going to be effective, and it definitely doesn't leave any room for conversation. Instead, you approach it this way:

I got the quarterly sales reports and saw that your numbers dropped by 20 percent last quarter. Is there something we can be doing to help better support you in your position?

Again, you owned the message, were specific about the details, and opened up a conversation to discuss the behaviors that led to the outcome. If Marcus was unresponsive, you could follow with,

I'm asking because last quarter your sales decreased by 20 percent, and I'd like to work with you to figure out why this happened, and what we can do to change that for the next quarter.

(It turns out that Marcus is struggling with the new CRM that was just rolled out and is missing opportunities. A quick training session and he's off and running.)

Even if you're giving positive feedback, it still needs to be specific and behavior-focused.

Studies show that when you give feedback based on someone's character instead of focusing it on a behavior, it can have the opposite of its intended impact. This is true for both positive and negative feedback.

Let's say Felicia's manager tells her all the time, "Wow. Felicia, you are so awesome. Felicia, you are just an awesome human being. Wow. Felicia, you're amazing. Felicia, amazing job."

The manager is thinking, "I am giving great, nice, positive reinforcement," but what Felicia's thinking is this, "Yeah, that feels nice, but I have no idea what I did that makes me awesome. I have no idea what I did specifically that made this be an awesome job. I don't have any specific feedback that tells me, keep doing X, Y, and Z."

Additionally, the pressure to remain "awesome" is high, and that can counter creativity.

With negative feedback, characterizing someone as "lazy" sets that as the expectation, or the norm. It doesn't encourage change from that status. In fact, it provides an internal scapegoat!

Always make sure your feedback follows this checklist: Own your message, avoid apology and generalizations, give feedback that is specific and behavior-focused, and make sure your words and your actions are synonymous.

After the Feedback: Mutual Understanding

Just because a conversation goes well, you can never assume both parties have the same understanding about what just happened. This is a fatal error many people make. A good rule is to always have a summary before departing any feedback conversation: "Summarize the steps you're going to take to do X." Remember, just because you say something doesn't mean it will be interpreted in the way you intended.

People do not interpret feedback in the same way. Just because you have a great feedback conversation does not mean you have mutual understanding until you check for it. Another good strategy is to document the feedback conversation in a summary email. That way both parties have a clear record of responsibilities and accountabilities.

⊙ ⊙ ⊙

In the next chapter, we'll talk about how you communicate to people above you, people below you, and people beside you. In other words, strategies you can use to communicate to people on all levels of the (real or perceived) hierarchy.

24

Message GPS

Your Communication Has a Direction,

and It Matters

Should you communicate with your investors the same way you would communicate with your BFF? Not if you want to get results!

Understanding the balance in communication with different people, including the different *perceived* hierarchical status of people, is important if you want to be truly dynamic and get results.

Upward Communication

If you're trying to get results when communicating to someone who is above you in status or perceives they are above you in status, you've got to cater to their ego. Let's be honest. If someone thinks they have (or legitimately does have) power over you, they will likely perceive their time as more important and valuable than yours. You don't need to kiss their ass, but you do need to cater to their ego a little.

But this isn't a bad thing! By catering to someone's ego, you can actually uncover more of what makes them tick. And by now you understand why that's important.

Here are the things you need to balance if you're communicating to someone higher in the food chain.

You need to *balance politeness with a clear task orientation*. You want to be cordial, but you don't want to waste time with small talk. You want to be polite: "Thanks for taking time to chat with me, Juan . . ." And you want to be specific and task-oriented: ". . . I want to talk to you about X, Y, and Z."

Boom.

You need to *balance friendliness with a respect for authority*. If someone perceives they have status over you, and you're trying to drive action, it's important to be friendly but confident, and balance it with a respect for their position. Respect their time and position, but also respect that you come to the table with ideas and perspectives that deserve to be recognized: "I really appreciate the way you encourage us to come forward with ideas. I have one I believe will make our hiring process and onboarding more seamless."

You need to *balance your own interest with company or investor needs*. If you're talking to a superior within the company or to an investor who has a stake in your company, they each have their own individual needs, but they also have the company's or portfolio's needs in mind.

REAL PEOPLE, REAL STORIES, REAL RESULTS

Jeffrey Hayzlett

CEO Hayzlett Group, C-Suite Network

Realize That Time Is Limited and Valuable

At the C-suite level, a lot of times you'll get calls, or emails, or requests, and they say, "Let's have coffee." Listen, dude, I don't have time for coffee. What is it you want? Every minute of my schedule, every minute of a C-suite executive's schedule is actually planned out for the day. Don't ask me for coffee, ask me for a specific thing. What is it

---

you'd like to get accomplished? Because usually I write back to people and say, "What is your agenda? What is the item you'd like?"

Do Your Due Diligence

Most people don't take the time to find out what is critical to me—to any executive. I don't care if they're Millennials, or baby boomers, or post-Depression-era adults. They just don't take the time. I really see a lot of people fail before they begin. Each C-suite has their own pain points. It could be growth. It could be margin. It could be both growth and margin. It could be customer satisfaction. There's a whole host of those, but you want to know what those are.

Get My Attention, Then Tell Me the Value

Most people over-present. They've got everything and the kitchen sink included in a presentation rather than being very succinct. You basically have eight seconds to hook me. What are you going to say that's so profound in the first eight seconds of this meeting that I want to hear the rest of the story? Don't tell me, "I work with this company." I couldn't care less. Who cares about that? What I do want to know is what value you're going to give to me. Really focus in on those two things: Get my attention, and then tell me the value.

Be Relentless, Be Compelling, Cause Things to Be Big Enough

"Well, they never got back to me." Of course they never got back to you. You haven't made it compelling enough for them to want to get back to you. You have to be relentless. You have to continually just go after it, go after it, and go after it. You have to be probing in your questions and the way in which you go at it to be able to get to the core of what they need to do, and show them you're going to add value.

Thinking Big, Acting Bigger

No matter how big you think you are, there's always someone bigger. The biggest communication mistake most people make is they limit themselves in terms of bragging about the things they have done, or do, or what they are, rather than just leaving it open. Once you stop doing this, and start thinking big and acting bigger, you'll realize there's a bigger world than that small, little world you think you're the king (or queen) of.

In this case, if you're communicating upward, it's important to be cognizant that no matter what communication, feedback, or results you're trying to get, you need to balance your wants and needs with the greater good: "Yes, implementing this idea would position me better to do X, but it will also result in increased profits in the third quarter."

Demonstrate a mutual benefit, and you'll proactively be on your way to the results you desire.

Downward Communication

Don't take your position of power for granted. The best leaders know how to manage each person as an individual and drive productivity through empowerment. If you're trying to get action from your employees, it's important to balance three things.

First, *balance personal respect with task accountability*. Employees really want to know, and this is true of all generations, that you recognize them as an individual. You want to have a personal level of respect for your employees. That often involves knowing something about them to emphasize respect for the individual's wants and needs. Then balance that personalization with direct accountability.

"I know you talked about really wanting to get involved with social media marketing in the company . . ."

That shows personal respect. Now here comes the accountability.

". . . if you're able to meet your sales goals next quarter, we'll look at getting you into a shadowing program so you can learn the social media ropes."

Next, *balance information gathering with existing data and analysis*. It's easy to look at an employee's client retention numbers, for example, and draw your own conclusions. That's a reactive mentality—I get data, I come to my own conclusion, and I react. Instead, come to the conversation with

>
>
> **FLASHBACK**
>
> Remember in Chapter 22 on equity we talked about how people work for rewards? Now we start to see how all these strategies can really combine to produce even more impact and encourage action.

a proactive mentality and gather information from the employee before drawing conclusions. Remember, dynamic communication is proactive!

If you begin the meeting by saying, "Your client retention is the lowest among the team. What's going on?", it isn't going to go over well. Not to mention that it breaks two of the key rules of providing feedback that we discussed in Chapter 23.

Instead, focus on getting the employee's perspective and input:

What resources do you feel would aid you in better retaining clients?

This opens the door to a conversation where the employee will tell you what he needs to do his job better. Or the employee will discuss the challenges of her role. In either situation, you'll discover valuable information that you likely wouldn't have learned if you had chosen the reactive approach.

Finally, you need to *balance listening with monitoring for complaints.* For many managers, this is a challenge. A lot of companies like to talk about having an "open door policy" where employees can come and say what's on their minds, but in reality the door needs to swing both ways.

You may have an open door policy as a manager, but you don't want to open a floodgate for complaints. If the conversation starts to shift toward a complaint, address it immediately. For example, if an employee comes to you complaining about her new supervisor, your shift from complaint to problem/solution could be:

> **SPOILER ALERT**
>
> In Chapter 25, we'll dive into specific strategies for complaint monitoring and encouraging a problem/ solution mentality with your staff.

I see you're frustrated about the reorganization process and you don't like your new supervisor. Let's talk about the specific things that are troubling you and what you've done to try to work on that relationship.

This way, if the employee is just complaining, she will probably drop the subject. If, on the other hand, she has a legitimate complaint and has tried a few strategies to no avail, you can get that information and help create a mutual solution.

Lateral Communication

Communicating with your friends, peers, colleagues, or counterparts is lateral communication. If you think in terms of organizational hierarchy, the people on the same horizontal level as you would be lateral. This type of communication often happens in work groups and teams. This communication can be difficult because there is no prescribed leader or power structure in place. But often, one party or the other assumes a higher role simply because of tenure within an organization. If we want to focus on driving action with lateral communication, here are a few things to keep in mind.

To manage lateral communication, focus on creating an equal exchange of value by *balancing a sense of equity with self-interest*. In order to grow relationships, you have to invest in them. At the peer-to-peer level, you identify the relative strengths of your communication partner. Often quid pro quo exchanges happen—if you can help cover my shift, I'll owe you one.

Acknowledge your communication history. What has been done or exchanged in the past? This is especially important if you're the one making the request and you've recently been asking for more favors.

> *I realize I've been asking for a lot of help with this new project. I appreciate your willingness to step forward and provide guidance. Please let me know when I can return the favor.*

Again, it's not depleting your resources—it's sharing your resources as an investment in a relationship. Lateral communication is all about investing in a relationship that benefits both of you, and helps the organization grow.

Balance listening supportively with responding. It's important to know how your lateral communication partner wants you to listen to them. In every situation, what your partner needs from you will be different. And often, asking how someone wants you to listen to them can both save time and strengthen the relationship: "Would you like me to listen and then provide ideas or feedback on this process, or do you just want to explain it to me now and ask for feedback at another time?"

This will give you all the information you need. You'll be able to listen supportively and also know what your expectations are in the conversation.

⊙ ⊙ ⊙

In the next chapter, we'll cover one way to help manage complaints and monitor your communication so you're driving people to find solutions and help solve their own problems.

Don't Be a Whiner

Be a Solution Provider

Nobody, at least no one I know, likes complainers—the people who always have something negative to say. The people who can find the one speck of dust in an otherwise spotless house and will never let you forget it. The people who go on and on about a problem but never do a darn thing to try to fix it.

Yeah, who likes them?

And in the workplace, constant complaints have negative consequences that reach into multiple areas of productivity, camaraderie, leadership, and culture. One bad apple *can* spoil the whole bunch.

This is why it's important to understand how to turn these bad apples into applesauce—in other words, how to turn complainers into problem solvers. Use the techniques presented in this chapter to help your employees better understand how to tackle problems (and yourself, should you be in a situation where you're reporting to someone).

Let's take it back to the playground again. You're in elementary school. It's recess time. You're playing foursquare with friends. You're

REAL PEOPLE, REAL STORIES, REAL RESULTS

Alan Weiss, Ph.D.

CEO and Founder, Summit Consulting

Know Your Starting Point

The ability to quickly diagnose what's going on is extraordinarily important, and people waste a lot of time. Often they try to place blame instead of find the cause, or they think they have a problem when they don't. They have a decision, so they get all tangled up in methodology, and the key is not to get tangled up in methodology. Where people get it wrong is they're confused about where they are. Making a decision, solving a problem, making a plan, innovating—these are all different starting points.

The Real Value Today Is in Innovation

Problem solving is fairly dull. Most companies are getting better and better at it. And it's fairly easy to do. There's an excellent methodology for problem solving because everything you know has already happened. You can find a problem's cause if you're disciplined and you know what to do. Innovation is raising the bar, so it's ambiguous and there's risk taking, and that's the key.

If You're 80 Percent Ready, Move

If you're resilient, you can make midcourse corrections, but if you're going to try to get every duck in a row and be perfect, it won't happen. You'll never get the ducks in a row; they'll just quack at you. And so if you wait for perfection, you will never get started. In fact, perfection is the greatest underminer of excellence I've ever seen in business.

No Buyer Cares About the Input

Methodology is an input. An output is a result. No buyer ever cares about the input. They care about the output. Instead of talking about a class or a program or a facilitation or an observation or coaching, you need to talk about better retention and

---

lower expenses and lower cost of acquisition and higher margins. That's what buyers want to hear, but people getting started continue to talk about what they do instead of what they create.

It's a Real Skill to Answer a Question Succinctly

This is a big mistake a lot of entrepreneurs make. Instead of telling people what they need to know, they tell them everything they know. So they ramble on, telling me things I don't need to hear, telling the prospect or the buyer things they don't need to hear because they feel they have to justify, justify, justify. So they give all the background on where it came from, they quote three Greek philosophers and talk about somebody else who did it and how they've improved on it, and by the time they're done, you don't know what to retain and what to forget, and it's exhausting. Identify the need. Match it with the value you provide. Bring that to the table.

---

passing the ball back and forth, bouncing it from square to square, following the standard rules of the game, and then all of a sudden one friend grabs the ball and says you lost. He made up a new rule on the fly.

How do you feel?

You're probably angry. So what are you going to do? You're going to try to get even.

Maybe you go up to your friend, grab the ball back, yell "Cheater!" and decide never to play with him again. Maybe you tell the playground monitor that your friend changed the rules midgame and that wasn't fair. Maybe you decide to let your friend win this time but vow to never talk to him again. Or maybe you pitch a fit and start crying. Again, you're a kid; that might be accepted.

But that won't fly in the workplace. Even if someone is cheating or treating you unfairly, you need to find a way to deal with it—or encourage your employees to deal with it—that results in a positive outcome for all involved.

Let's take that proverbial ball and transition it into taking the lead on a project team you and four others are assigned to. You were designated as the leader, but a teammate, Mario, is working hard to steal your thunder. You've tried addressing it with Mario, to no avail.

You want to be treated fairly, and you want to complain, but you know that won't get results. Running to your supervisor and saying, "Anna, you told me to take the lead on this project, but Mario stole it from me," is going to make you sound like a whiner, and someone who can't work well in teams. Instead, let's turn this complaint situation into an opportunity.

Instead, you go to your boss and say: "Anna, I'm excited to be working on this new project. The whole team is energized. In fact, Mario has started to take the lead on the project reporting and seems to be enjoying it. Is that OK with you? And, if so, what's something else I can take the lead on?" or "And, if so, is it OK if I take over the creative side of the project?"

See the difference? You're not complaining. You're stating the facts. You're presenting the problem. And then you're asking for help with figuring out a solution or presenting a possible solution. In fact, that's the three-step format for turning any complaint into a problem/solution presentation.

Step One: State the Relevant Facts

Present the facts needed for someone to understand the situation and provide any necessary context. If there are opinions involved, make sure you own them (think back to the section in Chapter 23 on feedback and owning your messages), but try to keep them at a minimum unless they are directly relevant to the problem at hand or the situation you want changed.

Step Two: Present the Situation or Problem

As in the example above, the fact was that Mario was taking over your assigned responsibility. The situation or problem is that you now have no clear responsibility and you need one. This step also involves outlining any measures you've taken to solve the problem yourself. For example, if you were trying to figure out the proper protocol for requesting professional development funds and you had already consulted the employee handbook and couldn't find the answer, you'd want to communicate that you had already taken that action. This demonstrates that you've been proactive in trying to find a solution yourself before coming to your supervisor.

Step Three: Ask for Help or Offer a Solution

Asking for help is not a sign of weakness, especially if you've already tried to help yourself (and you communicated that with the second step). Just make sure you're ready to act on the solution given to you. If you have a potential solution, this is where you present that for consideration.

You know, [supervisor], I really want to succeed on this project, but I don't feel I have the resources. I went to HR and asked for X, but they said it wasn't available. I also talked to [name] and he wasn't able to offer any insight. I'm kind of at a loss, can you help me?

You're stating the facts, noting that the problem exists, and saying what you've done to try to solve it on your own. Now you're asking for help. That's not a complaint. You found a problem, you tried solutions, now you need your manager's support. That's dynamic communication.

Reasonable vs. Incessant Complaints

You may have an open door policy as a manager, but you don't want to let it be a floodgate for complaints. But some complaints do have merit—they may just not be phrased well. You need to be able to distinguish between reasonable and incessant complaints. The decision to phrase something as a complaint is a communication choice. And sometimes, good people make poor communication choices.

> **FLASHBACK**
>
> A framework for organizing your solution that is based in psychology and shown to drive action and acceptance is found in Chapter 17. Also, we'll be covering a great framework to present your entrepreneurial ideas in Chapter 27.

For instance, in high-stress situations, employees who might otherwise bring solutions to the table may come to you with complaints. This is where distinguishing between reasonable and incessant complaints is important, as you don't want to devalue the contributions of a team member who is typically solution-oriented but is currently in a stressful situation. Here are some strategies for dealing with reasonable and incessant complaints.

For reasonable complaints, it is important to recognize what is being communicated and paraphrase it back to the person making the complaint. This demonstrates you're listening and ensures that you've reached a clear understanding of the problem and all the variables at play. If you do not feel you have a solid grasp of the situation, ask the necessary questions to clarify.

Incessant complaints are sometimes simply a cry for attention. You need to determine if this is the case, and if it is, why the employee is seeking attention in this way. Getting to the root of that problem is productive on multiple levels, as you not only can stop the endless complaint stream, but often identify root cause issues and quickly turn the conversation around.

Another way to deal with incessant complaints is to turn the complaint into a problem/solution opportunity. This puts the onus on the complainer to actually take responsibility for the situation—or at least recognize that he just wants to rant. In these situations, use the three steps outlined above to help your employee present the complaint in a different way.

> *OK, Xavier. I see you're upset about the new compensation plan.*
> *(Acknowledging that you heard)*
>
> *What are the specific aspects of the plan that frustrate you?*
> *(Getting to Step 1—stating the facts)*
>
> *These things are bothering you because . . .?*
> *(Addressing Step 2—presenting the problem)*
>
> *What do you think would be a better approach?*
> *(Encouraging Step 3—offering a solution)*

Complaints can derail productivity, impact morale, and slow progress. But they can also be a helpful warning sign for legitimate problems in your business. When you turn complaint situations into problem/solution opportunities, you get to the real causes behind the issues and move forward in a manner that benefits all involved.

⊙ ⊙ ⊙

In the next chapter, we'll talk about ways to retain your talented employees, including strategies for what not to say if you want to keep good people around. We'll also touch on ways to highlight people in a way that makes you look like a rock star for bringing the talent to the table.

Retain, Innovate, or Die

Strategies for Employee Retention and Development

You Better Recognize!

Retaining Talent and Highlighting Employees

Creating a culture that supports, encourages, and recognizes innovation is important. People want to be part of something bigger than themselves, and businesses that cater to this sense of belonging see increased employee buy-in. Businesses that look internally for solutions to problems, ideas for expansion, and processes for improvement make employees feel like an integral part of an organization and are more likely to retain top talent. Those that don't are headed the way of the dinosaur.

Turnover, and the inability to attract innovative employees, plagues many organizations and stunts business growth. Cultivating an environment that rewards entrepreneurial thinking—or intrapreneurship—is one key change a company can make that will help attract and keep proactive and forward-thinking employees.

Tips to Create a Culture of Innovation

These four tips will help your business implement new methods to put innovation in your company DNA.

Tip One: Provide Time and Space for Innovation

If you want employees to come up with new ideas, you need to give them time during standard business hours to create without penalty. One of the best-known examples of this practice is Google, which gives employees 20 percent of their work week to use for generating ideas for Google-related products and services.

Doing this communicates to employees that you value their time and insight—that you welcome their ideas and encourage them to be active participants in the organization. In turn, this produces a work environment where employees feel invested in the company and its success.

Tip Two: Generate a Process for Idea Submission

A mistake that many companies make is allowing time for innovation but then leaving employees wondering how to actually communicate their ideas. Providing employees with a process for submitting or pitching their ideas lets them know what information they should present and what research they should do, and gives direction for execution.

This framework can also reduce the time you spend evaluating ideas, as only those ideas that are a bit more fleshed out will make it to the presentation stage. (Note: This doesn't mean that quick, spur-of-the-moment ideas aren't valuable—in fact, sometimes they are the best ones. But providing a venue for those, separate from the formal pitch, is essential and perhaps a precursor to the presentation.)

> **SPOILER ALERT**
>
> Chapter 27 provides just this—a framework for submitting ideas to encourage your employees to think like an entrepreneur (hint: you can also use it as a framework for pitching contracts).

An example of a company that does this well is DreamWorks. At DreamWorks, employees at all levels can learn how to pitch an idea successfully—the program encourages creation from all employees, not matter their job role or title.

Tip Three: Reward the Process, not the Result

One surefire way to squash innovation is to penalize employees if their ideas don't work out. Do not view this as wasted time. Instead, view it as time when an employee was actively participating in improving the company. When you give employees permission to fail, they are willing to be more creative—more innovative and riskier—with their thinking. This can often lead to the best ideas. Consider creating awards for your employees that recognize creativity, innovation, and the thought process. Proctor & Gamble, for example, has a "heroic failure award" and Intuit holds "failure parties."

Tip Four: Respect the Individual Process

The concept of equifinality states that there are many paths to the same end—in business, that means there are multiple ways to reach a final goal. Think of navigating from San Francisco to New York City. There are many different paths you can take to get from one city to the other, and many different methods of transportation you could use. But in choosing one—say, a red-eye flight—you're missing out on the many other possible discoveries and sights that a combination flight and road trip would have presented.

If you're focusing on cultivating a culture of innovation and developing your employees, those potential discoveries and observations are key to growth. A fatal error that many managers make is assuming their ideas or processes are always the best and the most efficient. In organizations there are many ways to accomplish a single task. Yes, some may be more efficient than others, but often an employee's learning process in accomplishing a task is just as important as the task itself. Allow your employees space to learn. What they do with the lessons might surprise you.

Avoid These Phrases

Now that you know some basics, let's look at some specific communication messages you should avoid. If you want to keep the innovation engine humming and retain employees who are working hard to make your business better, here are some phrases you absolutely do not want to use.

Stick to Your Job. That's Not in Your Job Description

Want to make an employee feel she has no use beyond her immediate job description? This phrase kills any organizational buy-in and stops any incentive the employee has to think of ideas outside her immediate purview. This communicates to an employee that her thoughts have no value to the organization as a whole, and that the only thing that matters is her singular function.

Instead, ask questions:

How do you see this idea fitting in with your current charge?

How do you see this idea expanding your responsibilities?

How do you see this idea benefiting the organization as a whole?

Asking questions gets the employee to make the connections on her own, instead of you making them for her. It can also enhance your understanding of her vision and how it can contribute to the greater organizational mission. This will help you put the right people in the right places to maximize skills and increase inter-team collaboration.

We Don't Have the Resources

When you tell an employee this, you're also communicating that his idea isn't worth exploring or his contribution isn't good enough to warrant consideration. Managers who want to increase innovation find a way to provide resources for promising and invested employees, or encourage the employee to find the resources himself. They also know creativity thrives in the face of constraint and will reframe the negative response into a thought-fueling competition.

Instead of saying "We don't have the resources," issue a challenge.

I don't have the resources immediately at my disposal to approve this today; however, why don't we think of a couple of ways we could rearrange our priorities to make your idea a possibility?

I like this idea and want to think about how it fits into our overall strategy a bit more. Come up with a few solutions for how we could integrate this idea within our current operational plan, and let's meet tomorrow to discuss.

These alternatives let the employee know that you do value the idea and you want to consider how it could come to fruition. They also encourage the employee to invest more time in his idea, which will increase buy-in to the organization and your leadership.

That's Not the Way We Do Things Here

Want to make a new employee feel like an outsider? Use this phrase. Telling an employee she doesn't know how things are done communicates two negative things: that she doesn't know the organization well, and that outside ideas, perspectives, and innovations are not welcome. It also is exclusive messaging, positioning this employee as part of the "out group" as discussed in Chapter 21.

Although organizations have rules and policies, that doesn't mean they should never be re-examined. Maybe now is the time and this is the place to do that. Instead, try encouraging integration.

In the past, we've approached this idea from an XYZ perspective. However, I think this new idea has promise. Let's see how we can integrate your solution with our existing operations to improve the organization as a whole.

Last time we attempted this implementation it didn't work, but we now have new people in place and new products on the market. Organize a meeting with your peers and see how we could approach this process differently from your perspective. I look forward to hearing your findings.

You can also challenge the employee to think of those means of integration and bring possible solutions to you for a conversation using the framework laid out in Chapter 25.

REAL PEOPLE, REAL STORIES, REAL RESULTS

John Lee Dumas

CEO, Founder, and Host, *Entrepreneur on Fire*

Learn by Highlighting the Talents of Others

When I started *EOFire*, I thought, "I don't have much value to add to entrepreneurs." But I realized I could create a platform. I could create a medium of communication where I could bring amazing people on and give them a microphone and a megaphone to share their thoughts, their message, their mission with the world, and personally learn from them and, eventually, become that entrepreneur that has value to share.

Amplify Your Strengths

If you don't spend time amplifying your strengths and instead are running around doing things you're crappy at, you're wasting time, energy, bandwidth, and focus. That's not going to allow you to grow a great business. Don't try to become OK at something you're crappy at, because nobody wants "OK" anyway. So bring in somebody who's great at it and build a team.

Have a Mentality of Service

If you help enough other people succeed, then you'll always have as much success as you want. That, to me, is such an inspiring motto, saying, "How can I build you up? How can I help you?" People having that mentality make this world go around. That's where the people really do rise to the top, always having that attitude and mentality of service and saying, "How can I benefit you going that way?" instead of thinking, "How is this going to eventually come around and help me?"

Highlight People at All Levels Who Display Talent in Different Ways

Crushing it means different things to different people. For *EOFire*, the best of the best doesn't mean we interview the people who are making the most money or who have the biggest audience. I love showcasing people who are crushing it, making $3,000, $4,000 a month doing what they love and growing their community slowly, strongly. It's a very passionate living that they're creating because that is their love.

The Curse of Knowledge

The goal of *EOFire* is to share the journey of its guests. They think back to their worst entrepreneurial moment, their biggest a-ha moment, and talk about the process from day one. A lot of people forget what it was like to be at the beginning. When people are asking for advice, they don't go back to a place of, "Where are you right now? Let's figure out where you are. Let me think where I was then, and build you up." Instead, it's this huge dichotomy and it just doesn't work. I call that the curse of knowledge.

Not Being Transparent Is the Biggest Communication Mistake You Can Make

A lot of people claim transparency, but they're not quite there. Everything you're doing is communication. Whether it's a picture, whether it's video, audio, whatever it might be, you're communicating to your audience. Don't just show the good times and communicate those things, but show the full circle. Your audience will really appreciate it.

Now you know how to set up a culture to encourage entrepreneurial thinking and the messages to avoid discouraging innovation. But how can you recognize and highlight employees who are doing a stellar job? In so many ways!

Recognizing and Highlighting Awesomeness

According to a poll conducted by the Maritz Institute, employees who are recognized on the job are more likely to feel valued, stay with the company longer, invest in the company by going above and beyond, and feel a complete commitment to the organization. And not just a little—at least five to 11 times more likely. Clearly, this is something we need to be doing!

We learned in Chapter 22 that people work for rewards. Recognizing your employees for their hard work and contributions is important to the overall health of your business. Also, when you provide someone with recognition, you'll often get greater results not only from them but from the remainder of the team as well, as they will be motivated to work toward that same type of recognition.

As a reminder, recognition can take different forms; it doesn't always have to be in a grand public forum. In general, though, if you're going to use information, a process, a procedure, or an idea from an employee, it is always good to give credit where credit is due. And if you're a business that doesn't yet have employees, you can use these strategies with your clients, too.

Free or Low-Cost Recognition Ideas

Here are some ideas for communicating recognition to your employees that cost little to no money. I'm going to start with my absolute favorite, which I find is rarely used.

Handwritten Notes or Cards

When's the last time you got a handwritten note or card saying "thank you" for something? I can tell you exactly when mine was. It was about three weeks ago from a client thanking me for speaking at their event. They paid me, and they thanked me. Amazing! (True to who I am, I had already sent them a handwritten thank-you note for inviting me to share with their employees.) Even a simple handwritten sticky note on an employee's computer can make a big difference. Try it. You'll feel great. And your employees will, too.

Feature on Website and in Social Media

It doesn't have to be major, but it adds flair to your company and highlights your culture. Plus, who doesn't want to share how awesome they are? And it's great for your employees to be able to link to social proof in their LinkedIn profiles. Another way to do this is to enable employees to tell their stories of working at your company and the difference they make. You can structure the messaging like this: "Every day the people who make up Awesome Business XYZ are making the world a better place. Here are just some of the many ways our teams impact the community."

If you don't have employees, consider interviewing other people to build your credibility and expertise for finding good people, even though they don't work for you. People will build a tribe around you because you earn a reputation for finding smart people that add value to a show.

Take our spotlight interview for this chapter, John Lee Dumas, who built an empire by highlighting the stories of others in his podcast, *Entrepreneur on Fire*. People like hearing stories of success. They give us hope and inspiration. They give us something to aspire to. Stories also drive action.

Name Something After an Employee

Whether it be a product, a service package, a conference room, an award, a program, etc., this is a fun and inexpensive honor. (When I visited BuzzFeed for the first time, their conference rooms were all named after famous internet cats. How fun!) You can have a cool unveiling in a team meeting, reinforcing the employee's contribution and giving them public recognition. Or you can let the employee choose the name for something (within reason, of course). Either way, it's an enjoyable way to say "great work."

Have Random and Fun Awards

Not everything in business needs to be about bottom line numbers and results. Create unique awards that highlight great things employees are doing or their contributions to the office. "The Fastest Email Responder." "The Early Bird." "The Best Birthday Celebrator." "The Best Idea That Crashed and Burned." "The Most Creative Use of Paper Clips." Whatever it is, personalize it, and follow it up with a handwritten note of thanks.

Your business wouldn't exist without multiple communities of people. Even if you don't have employees yet, your communities consist of vendors, contractors, and other partners. Use these strategies to foster innovation, and you'll create a supportive network that grows with you as you grow your business.

⊙ ⊙ ⊙

In the final chapter, we'll talk about instituting a framework for innovation in the workplace to encourage your intrapreneurs to come forward with well-thought-out ideas. As hinted at earlier in this chapter, you can also use this framework to think about creating the best possible pitch to a client.

Six Steps for Innovation

Cultivating Intrapreneurship

n creating a culture of innovation within an organization, you want to make sure you have the ability to not only highlight people and bring their ideas to the surface, but also have a process in place so you can escalate those ideas up the chain to get action taken. Creating systems for intrapreneurship is a key success factor in many of today's successful companies. An intrapreneur is someone who thinks like an entrepreneur but is an employee within an organization. They get that steady paycheck, but they want to bring ideas to the surface. They're not happy just sitting there with the status quo, and they want to know they can impact decisions and the trajectory of the business. (An entrepreneur, on the other hand, is a person who starts their own business but also assumes any financial risk that goes along with that.) Your intrapreneurs are entrepreneurial thinkers that drive organizational change and are motivated by creation. Squashing attempts at innovation is an easy way to kill employee morale and experience high-talent turnover.

To avoid this, look at developing an internal process that *all* employees can use to bring ideas to the table and communicate them to the right people within your organization. This will encourage your intrapreneurs to contribute and think about ways to make the business better.

Here is a six-step blueprint you can use to help your employees develop their ideas. Adapt it to your business as necessary. But these six steps will help guide you to creating a process where well-thought-out, well-researched, and well-positioned ideas will come to the surface. Not only will ideas come to you in a more actionable format, but you'll be professionally developing your employees and giving them skills that will live on long beyond their current role—creating a great employee experience. And that's something they'll thank you for later. (And if you're a solopreneur, don't stop reading! You can use these six steps to help you create better pitches to potential clients. Just reframe the language a little, and you'll be well on your way to more sophisticated proposals.)

Step One: Identify—Know Your Audience

Your employees should know to whom they can bring ideas. Do you have a hierarchy, or can they go straight to the top? Define this process.

The first step in any successful communication is to know your audience. Help your employees know their audience when it comes to presenting ideas. These are some questions they will be asking if you don't point them in the right direction. Or you can just have them ask these questions and decide to whom they should present an idea.

- ⊙ Who are the people in the organization to whom you should pitch your idea?
- ⊙ Who has the power to make your idea come to fruition?
- ⊙ Who has the power to assign resources to help you make your idea a reality?

Step Two: Match—Is This the Right Fit/Place/Time?

Have criteria to help your employees evaluate if their idea is the right fit for your organization. This starts with having a clearly defined mission, vision, values, and purpose (MVVP) statement that is communicated through the organization (and, really, throughout everything you do).

- ⊙ Does your idea fit the mission, vision, values, or purpose of the organization?
- ⊙ Does your idea fit a need the company has?
- ⊙ Does your idea fit a need the customers have?
- ⊙ Does your idea fit a need the organization has internally?

If an idea isn't an obvious fit with the MVVP of the company, you'll need to find a way to rethink it so it does fit. You want to make sure there's some connection between the two. If not, you need to flesh out some other ideas to get those connections there. It's just like when you're teaching someone a leadership skill: You want leaders whose actions and words are synonymous. If your idea and the values of an organization are not synonymous, it's not going to be enacted.

For example, on the surface the idea to start designing wearable technology may not fit with a culinary supplies company. However, if the idea aligns with the MVVP of the company and can solve a problem customers have (let's say, wearable technology that helps keep track of the timing of multiple dishes and buzzes you for reminders to stir, flip, decrease temperature, etc.), then there might be a fit.

Step Three: Evaluate—Ideas, Ideas, and More Ideas

Often when teams get together to brainstorm ideas, the tendency is to stick to ideas that have already worked, not challenge the status quo. This is part of the phenomenon known as groupthink. That is not always a bad thing, but it does mean you're potentially missing out on other great ideas if you're not encouraging innovation.

Once someone has an idea, knows the audience who will consider the idea, and believes the idea is the right match for an organization, it's time to evaluate the idea further and see if it can be even better. Before coming forward with an idea, consider running it through a handful of other questions to help evaluate and strengthen it.

REAL PEOPLE, REAL STORIES, REAL RESULTS

Ekaterina Walter

Wall Street Journal Bestselling Author, *Think Like Zuck*

The Most Important Things Around Innovation Are Very Basic

It's focusing on people and culture, it's hiring the right team members, it's finding people who are very passionate about what you do so that the fit within building that culture happens continuously. Passion trumps everything. The skill sets and knowledge about the business and the product can be taught. Passion can't. Passion leads to innovation.

Partner Where You Can Create a Successful Ecosystem for Your Business

Make sure you partner with the right people, internally and externally, in building that network of success. Key things really always come down to fundamentals. Have a great team, trust your team to do the best, and make sure you put really smart people in leadership because leadership can break or make the company. Ask people for advice but then be willing to listen. If that happens, you're going to be so much more, and innovation cycles will just start popping up.

Approach Your Employees in Terms of Relationship, Not Dictatorship

Having a leader or leaders on an executive team really truly understand that they don't know everything is crucial to innovation. It's ego vs. humility. A lot of founders are so centered on how awesome they are and how fantastic their product is that all they want to do is talk. When you listen and when you put your ego in your pocket and zip it up and just sit there and observe the conversations happening around you about your product, about your company, opportunities and ideas come.

Not Hoarding Information Helps You Harness Collective Knowledge and Build Trust

Transparency and passion married together builds teams that are going to be loyal and going to be there for you, and they will innovate the heck out of . . . even in places you don't expect them to innovate.

Mark Zuckerberg at Facebook holds town halls regularly. The only request is that information shared openly and transparently does not leave the room. As soon as information starts leaking, they'll stop holding those. They stand in front of their employees and talk. Zuckerberg is great about it. He answers questions openly. He talks about what he's thinking about, potential approaches, what he knows about the industry. I've seen so many people take less salary to work for teams and cultures that really, truly trust them, that bring them in and say, "Look, here are the problems. Help us solve them." And then they listen to those people.

It's Not About the Product, It's About the Experience

How are you creating movements around your brand, around your industry, around your products to a point, but your products are part of your bigger self, your bigger culture, your bigger company? How are you building movements to where people will want to come back, where they'll want to have a relationship with you? You do it through experiences. It's all about experience management. Your product does not matter. What matters is the level of experience you provide your customers.

Sometimes you'll find an even stronger idea emerges as a result, or you become even more confident in your original concept. Either way, it's a win. Here are some questions you can use, or create your own using these as a springboard.

- ⊙ If you had implemented this idea six months ago, what would the organization look like now?
- ⊙ If you asked five other people in the company how to solve the problem your idea fixes, what would they have to say?
- ⊙ If you were evaluating this idea from the perspective of [insert person, business, or other entity], how might it change? (For example, Disney, Google, Steve Jobs, Shaq, ET, Frank Underwood, etc.)
- ⊙ If you break your idea into three micro ideas and pick the most important one, what would it be?
- ⊙ If you had to explain your idea to a kindergartener, how would you do it? (This helps someone see whether their idea is more complex than it needs to be.)

Step Four: Gather—Get Buy-In and Support

Most ideas do not manifest, nor do they come to fruition, in isolation. And ideas need people to enact them and make them work. So far we've thought of everything in terms of the audience that will hear your idea and the organizational fit. Now it's time to look at the idea from the perspective of the people who will actually benefit from, use, or implement the idea.

You can have the most brilliant idea in the world, but if the people who are going to be enacting or implementing the idea don't do it well, your idea is going to fall flat, you are going to be judged for it, and you won't see the fruits of your labor. Getting buy-in on multiple levels is really important.

Let's look at an example. Say you are an engineer at a software development company. You know consumer feedback is important, but it's not getting to you accurately all the time because the customer service reps aren't documenting well enough. You have an idea to get the customer service team iPads so they can take notes more efficiently and immediately upload them into the company cloud. But if you take this idea to the top without getting buy-in from customer service reps, you may not get great implementation. It's important to talk to the people who will actually be using, implementing, or acting on your idea, because if you don't have their buy-in, success may not happen.

You want to be able to say something like this:

I've talked to many of our customer service reps about getting more detailed reports on customer experiences. They tell me they can't write things down fast enough. If they had a way to record a conversation while simultaneously taking notes or highlighting things, that would be really beneficial and enable us to provide better customer service.

Step Five: Analyze—Know Your Position, Situation, and Attributes

A lot of people have heard of a SWOT analysis—strengths, weaknesses, opportunities, and threats. This is a pretty solid framework for analyzing your ideas, and I definitely suggest it.

But when it comes to bringing ideas forward in an organization, especially if you want to be the one to take responsibility for the idea, you should be doing a SWOT analysis not just on the idea, but on *you*.

I call this a P-SWOT, or a Positioning SWOT. Give me one last geeky professor moment.

In the 1960s and 1970s, a management consultant at the Stanford Research Institute named Albert Humphrey came up with a way to improve corporate planning. He thought, "There has to be a better way to analyze plans so we can see what needs to be fixed before we execute" (or something like that—I'm paraphrasing here). Thus SWOT analysis was born. Since then, it's been taught in most business programs and is used in many businesses.

You need to evaluate your strengths, weaknesses, opportunities, and threats when it comes to your being in a position to spearhead this idea or present it in the first place. Think about the characteristics, perspectives, experiences, and skills that make you the right fit to execute the proposal. In other words, how are you positioning yourself to be the right person for the job? Here are some questions you can ask for each part.

Strengths
- Why should you be the one to make this idea happen?
- What skills do you bring to the table that will ensure its success?
- What is your personal investment in the success of this idea?

Weaknesses
- Do you have the necessary time to complete this idea?
- Do you have the necessary resources to bring the idea to life?
- What skills are you lacking that would help increase the rate of success?
- What experiences in the past would prohibit you from succeeding in the present?

Opportunities
- What opportunities beyond this idea exist if it's implemented successfully?

- What can you learn from others who have implemented similar ideas?
- What are some opportunities to expand this idea?
- What personal opportunities might come if you execute well?

Threats

These are the internal and external factors that can become problematic before, during, or after the execution of your plan.

- What is standing in the way of you making this idea work?
- Are there others in the organization who would oppose this idea?
- Do any of your weaknesses leave you vulnerable to threats?
- What internal and external factors to your business exist that may threaten success?
- What internal and external factors to yourself exist that may threaten success?

Step Six: Craft and Deliver—Message, Channel, Pitch

We're finally here! The final step. Now your employees have a killer idea ready to bring to you for consideration. Have a way for employees to design and deliver their ideas that makes sense for you and your business. Here are some considerations for you to think about when designing this step.

- How should the pitch be delivered?
- Through what channel(s) do you want it communicated?
- What documentation do you want to accompany the idea?
- Who should be included in the conversation?

You might want to also consider setting expectations for when a pitch will be received and evaluated, and when a decision will be made. Another strategy is to create an "application" process that will filter out pitches and ideas that aren't fully developed. To help get better ideas, develop mentorship programs to help employees flesh out their ideas and pitches. Finally, a way to encourage innovation and intrapreneurship is to schedule monthly all-hands-type meetings where everyone can listen to selected ideas, setting the bar and motivating through observation.

No matter what you do, it's important to create a process that sets employees up for success so that those who bring ideas forward aren't punished if the idea doesn't work. As we discussed in Chapter 26, innovation dies when people are afraid to create and invent because of potential negative consequences.

⊙ ⊙ ⊙

In the next . . . wait—that's the last of the strategy chapters. Holy cow, that went by fast. Now let's wrap it up with some thoughts on how you can make the most out of what you've learned.

Slapping a Bandage on It Doesn't Work

When companies hire a trainer to come in and present a session in isolation, thinking it will solve a problem, I call this "The Bandage Syndrome," because you're merely slapping a bandage on the situation, hoping it heals itself. Training may help solve an immediate need, but as soon as it gets a little wet, the bandage falls off and is no longer useful.

It's just like buying a book, or even reading the book. Until you make actionable plans to apply what you've learned, the book is a mere bandage. The same thing happens after a great workshop, idea-generating conference, or awesome brainstorming session.

I'll admit it: I've done what I'm about to tell you *not* to do. It's easy to fall into this trap. But you're not going to do it this time. And neither am I.

How many times have you read a book, watched a YouTube video, seen someone do something awesome, attended a training session, and thought: "I'm going to do/change/model this in my business?"

And then you don't.

It's not that you intentionally didn't follow through, but this thing called life got in the way (or Netflix just released the new *House of Cards* season. I get it—binge watching is cheaper than therapy). Whatever the reason, despite your best intentions, what you learned dissipated and never got implemented. This happens all the time.

But not this time.

You know why? Because we've made an action plan together, that's why. This book cames with a workbook to plan out how you're going to implement the strategies you learned in this book into your business so you can be more dynamic. And if you didn't already use the free workbook to help you, go to www.dynamiccommunicationbook.com now and get it. Let's do it!

The Law of Diminishing Marginal Motivation

In college, I took an economics course. I wasn't a business major; it just sounded fun. Yes, I was one of those people. One principle I remember vividly is the law of diminishing marginal utility. In short, this law means that the first time you consume something, it has more utility than the second time you consume it, and so on.

My college economics professor explained it this way: "Imagine you are hungry and you eat a cheeseburger." (Which wasn't hard; I was hungry, and I like cheeseburgers.)

"That first cheeseburger has a lot of utility. Then you decide to eat a second cheeseburger. That second cheeseburger isn't going to be as satisfying or useful as the first, because some of the utility is no longer needed."

Why am I talking about cheeseburgers?

Because the law of diminishing marginal utility also comes into play when you're excited about a new idea, concept, theory, person, etc. I call it the law of diminishing marginal motivation.

When you first learn a new idea, it's exciting. When you learn how this idea can change something in your life for the better, it's even more exciting. You're motivated. You're eager.

But the further you get from putting that idea on paper and making a plan, the less likely you are to follow through on implementing it. Your motivation declines, especially when another new idea is presented. Or you implement one idea, and forget about the rest of the great strategies that you learned. That's the law of diminishing marginal motivation in action. Here's how we aren't going to fall prey to this law.

Write It. Do It. Celebrate It.

Did you know that by writing down your idea by hand, as opposed to typing it or just thinking about it, you're creating up to 10,000 new neural pathways? That's why hand writing your goals, notes, etc., is important to learning and goal accomplishment. Plus, who doesn't want more neural pathways? That just sounds sexy.

That's why, at the beginning of this book, I told you to write down one thing—just one—from each chapter that you want to act on and apply. Now's the time to revisit that list of ideas. Note which ones you've already started to implement, and which you haven't. Make a plan for applying each idea that is time-specific. This way you'll have an action plan to make sure that these knowledge cheeseburgers provide a high amount of utility.

Now that you've written all this down, created new neural pathways, and understood how to turn these ideas into a positive shift in your business—and your life—you're ready to exercise dynamic communication and grow, lead, and manage your business.

I'm a big believer in celebrating success. Heck, when writing each chapter of this book I had a minicelebration upon completion. And, though now I'm putting the cart before the proverbial horse, the celebration that shall happen upon the book's release . . . I'm already getting excited!

Especially if more than one person is involved in making an idea become reality (and since we don't exist in a vacuum, chances are you'll have people helping or supporting you along the way), celebrating success is just one way to bring people together, remind them of the bigger picture, and thank them for their contributions.

Conclusion / Slapping a Bandage on It Doesn't Work

So help me help you celebrate the successes you experience as a result of the strategies you learned in this book! Instagram, tweet, or Facebook me @dynamicjill your picture with the book, or with one of your handwritten takeaways from a chapter, and I'll share some celebration love with you.

Are you ready to grow, lead, and manage your business? Now that you're armed with these 27 strategies, you're ready to roll. We are no longer getting dynamic.

Let's *be* dynamic.

Index